TO

FROM

DATE

CREATED FOR *Compassion*

KINDNESS IN THE CULTURE

DEVOTIONAL GUIDE

TONY EVANS

DEAR READER,

God is compassionate and kind. It's who He is. He gives us the food we eat, the sunshine we enjoy, and the air we breathe. Not only does His kindness allow us an existence with majestic mountains, sandy beaches, and breathtaking sunsets, but it also provides us with the ability to appreciate the beauty and wonder of His creation. And His kindness doesn't stop there. We also experience it through His forgiveness of our sins, His unconditional love for us, and His guidance toward righteousness. It is through His kindness that we can find hope, comfort, and strength no matter what circumstances we may face.

Now here's the question: Are we experiencing God's kindness and sharing it with others? Or are we keeping it to ourselves? God wants His family, His church, to be leaders in expressing His kindness to others. God wants us to glorify Him by doing good works in His name. God desires us to spread the kindness that He shows us to everyone we come across.

It's true—kindness isn't always our first response when we encounter the harshness of this world, but it is my hope that this devotional guide will help us tap into a well of God-given compassion that has the power to move mountains in our divisive social landscape. Together we can change the atmosphere of our communities for good.

Each entry includes:

- Scriptures for diving into God's Word
- A "Live It Out" message from me to encourage you on your kindness journey
- Reflection questions for personal growth
- A challenge to apply compassion in practical ways in your daily life

You might think that you are just one person whose light won't make that much of a difference. The truth is, your light matters. And when you choose God's way, you get God's strength and God's ideas on how to love. You and He are a force for good. My prayer for you as you use this guide is that you'll discover even more of what you were created for. Together we can be an army on His side, fighting for compassion and kindness in a world that desperately needs it.

For His kingdom,

Tony Evans

Dr. Tony Evans

Scan here for a group leader's guide.

For more from Dr. Tony Evans, go to *TonyEvans.org* or download his sermons on the Tony Evans Sermons app.

CONTENTS

DAY 01

To Glorify

Each of you should use whatever gift you have received to serve others, as faithful stewards of God's grace in its various forms.
I PETER 4:10 NIV

The King will reply, "Truly I tell you, whatever you did for one of the least of these brothers and sisters of Mine, you did for Me."
MATTHEW 25:40 NIV

Give to everyone who asks you, and from someone who takes your things, don't ask for them back.
LUKE 6:30 CSB

Give to him who asks of you, and do not turn away from him who wants to borrow from you.
MATTHEW 5:42

Suppose a brother or a sister is without clothes and daily food. If one of you says to them, "Go in peace; keep warm and well fed," but does nothing about their physical needs, what good is it?
JAMES 2:15-16 NIV

Pure and undefiled religion in the sight of our God and Father is this: to visit orphans and widows in their distress, and to keep oneself unstained by the world.
JAMES 1:27

And do not neglect doing good and sharing, for with such sacrifices God is pleased.
HEBREWS 13:16

Father, I want those you gave Me
To be with Me, right where I am,
So they can see My glory, the
splendor You gave Me,
Having loved Me
Long before there ever was a world.
JOHN 17:24 THE MESSAGE

LIVE IT OUT

The Bible calls us to do good works. And a lot of the time, when we hear the word *works*, we think *things*. But good works are not good things. You don't have to be a Christian to do good things. A person who doesn't even believe in God can build a hospital or an orphanage, help sick people, be a philanthropist, or mentor kids. But only Christians can do good works.

A *good work* is a divinely authorized activity that benefits somebody else in need, for which God gets the glory, and for which you do not expect a return.

A sinner can do good things, but he or she is not obligated to attach God to it. The person can do it and tell you he doesn't believe in God because God is not the motivating factor. Humanitarianism, maybe. A love for mankind may be the driver. But as Matthew 5:16 puts it, "Let men see your good works and glorify your Father who is in heaven." Not glorify "their" father, but glorify "your" Father, because you are doing the good things [or the good works] in His name.

To *glorify* means to advertise or put on display. So as Christians, we are not just supposed to do good things. In fact, you and I will get a letter in the mail, or a knock on the church door, from someone asking us to do things, and they say, "Don't attach God to it, okay? We want you to do this good thing, but we don't want the divine attachment." Well, that's a good thing, not a good work. God recognizes good works that He is attached to.

Additionally, good works are those for which we don't demand anything in return. Luke 6:30-31 says, "Give to everyone who asks you, and whoever takes away whatever is yours, do not demand it back. Treat others in the same way you want them to treat you."

When you do a good work, that is, something that is divinely authorized, that benefits somebody else in need in a way that attaches it to God without demanding anything in return, what you have done is gotten God's undivided attention.

REFLECTIONS

What is the difference between good things and good works? Write down some examples of when you've witnessed good things and when you've witnessed good works.

Think of a time when you have been served by someone. Write about how you knew that God was at the heart of it. How did that experience differ from other times when nice things were done for you?

Describe a time when glorifying God factored into your desire to show kindness to others.

In which scenarios have you found yourself happy to do something without anything in return? In which scenarios are you more likely to want someone to repay your kindness?

"

A GOOD WORK IS A DIVINELY AUTHORIZED ACTIVITY THAT BENEFITS SOMEBODY ELSE IN NEED, FOR WHICH GOD GETS THE GLORY, AND FOR WHICH YOU DO NOT EXPECT A RETURN.

CHALLENGE

Remember that a *good work* is a divinely authorized activity that benefits somebody else in need, for which God gets the glory, and for which you do not expect a return. It's completely natural for us to want both credit and payment for our good intentions. But when we invite the Holy Spirit into the process, He prepares our hearts to see situations and people with His eyes and His heart.

Spend some time in prayer this week, and ask to see things the way He does. It may be a brand-new idea for you to look for people to serve in His name, or it may be your modus operandi to pay it forward. Either way, find someone to serve. Do it in a way that God's presence is undeniable. If you're worried about wanting credit or gratitude, do it anonymously. Just make sure that before you walk away, the person on the receiving end knows a little more about God's love than they did before they met you.

You are the salt of the earth; but if the salt has become tasteless, how can it be made salty again? It is no longer good for anything, except to be thrown out and trampled under foot by men. You are the light of the world. A city set on a hill cannot be hidden; nor does anyone light a lamp and put it under a basket, but on the lampstand, and it gives light to all who are in the house. Let your light shine before men in such a way that they may see your good works, and glorify your Father who is in heaven.
MATTHEW 5:13-16

He said to them, "Go into all the world and preach the good news to all creation."
MARK 16:15 NIV

He must become greater;
I must become less.
JOHN 3:30 NIV

Now to Him who is able to do immeasurably more than all we ask or imagine . . . be glory.
EPHESIANS 3:20-21 NIV

DAY 02

Wealth in Works

So you see, faith by itself isn't enough. Unless it produces good deeds, it is dead and useless.
JAMES 2:17 NLT

For just as the body without the spirit is dead, so also faith without works is dead.
JAMES 2:26 CSB

But someone may well say, "You have faith and I have works; show me your faith without the works, and I will show you my faith by my works."
JAMES 2:18

For we are God's handiwork, created in Christ Jesus to do good works, which God prepared in advance for us to do.
EPHESIANS 2:10 NIV

Do your best to present yourself to God as one approved, a workman who does not need to be ashamed and who correctly handles the word of truth.
II TIMOTHY 2:15 NIV

For it is God who is working in you to will and to act according to His good purpose.
PHILIPPIANS 2:13 CSB

May [God] give you the power to accomplish all the good things your faith prompts you to do.
II THESSALONIANS 1:11 NLT

Whatever you do, work at it with all your heart, as working for the Lord, not for human masters, since you know that you will receive an inheritance from the Lord as a reward. It is the Lord Christ you are serving.
COLOSSIANS 3:23-24 NIV

LIVE IT OUT

You want to make God smile? Be rich in good works. Place value not on money or things, but on the wealth of good works you do. You will garner God's attention and super-size His presence in your life, which is wonderful! But in order to do that, you will have to set up margins in your life where it is possible to do good works.

You see, if you spend everything you have on yourself, then you won't have anything to do good works with. If you spend all your time on yourself, then you won't have time to give to any good works. If you spend all your talent on yourself, then you won't have any talent left over to share in good works with somebody else.

The word *good* means beneficial. And work is something you do, not just something you give.

Therefore, when we are called to good works, God is not just asking for a swipe of the credit card. He is asking for time, talent, and energy. Good works involve, well, *work*. To do good works for someone often means you've got to take off your suit and put on some jeans. To do good works means sometimes you have to take off the dress shirt and put on a T-shirt. When you get so high that you can't go low, then you have gotten too big for your spiritual britches.

When God says to be rich in good works, He is asking us to be generous with more than money. You may write a check, but don't let that check get you out of the work. In many places, the rich pay the check, and the poor do the work. But that creates a gap with God because He wants to know how much of your wealth lies in your good works.

REFLECTIONS

1 Write about a time when you've seen a financially wealthy person step in and do the hard work.

2 How does it make you feel when you see a senior pastor, company president, or another leader do work that might be considered menial or "below" them?

3 Write about a time when you felt a specific job or task was beneath you. What did God teach you through this experience?

4 Do you know someone who regularly shows up to help, no matter what the task at hand? What type of characteristics do they have?

5 Consider your own situation. Does your wealth tend to lie more in your checkbook or in your good works?

"

THE WORD GOOD MEANS BENEFICIAL. AND WORK IS SOMETHING YOU DO, NOT JUST SOMETHING YOU GIVE.

CHALLENGE

There's absolutely nothing wrong with financially supporting a need. That is a huge and necessary part of the good work that is being done around the world, and it is a kingdom principle to share what we have. But we can't stop there if we want to experience the fullness of God's pleasure and presence. Doing good works increases our joy because it increases the attention of the kingdom.

Find somewhere to apply your own elbow grease. It could be anything: serving meals at a homeless shelter, ringing a Salvation Army bell, mentoring a young person, taking a meal to an elderly neighbor, or asking a frazzled mom how you can serve her today. Ask the Lord to spark your creativity and to place real needs in front of you that you can meet. Try keeping a good works journal, not for the sake of keeping track of your own accolades but for recording where and how God partners with you to make a difference in others' lives. It might just change your own life, too.

The Lord doesn't see things the
way you see them. People judge
by outward appearance, but
the Lord looks at the heart.
I SAMUEL 16:7 NLT

Whoever wants to be a leader
among you must be your servant,
and whoever wants to be first among
you must become your slave.
MATTHEW 20:26-27 NLT

The joy of the Lord is your strength.
NEHEMIAH 8:10 NIV

For I can do everything through
Christ, who gives me strength.
PHILIPPIANS 4:13 NLT

Do to others whatever you would like
them to do to you. This is the essence of all
that is taught in the law and the prophets.
MATTHEW 7:12 NLT

Treasure Storage

Instruct those who are rich in this present world not to be conceited or to fix their hope on the uncertainty of riches, but on God, who richly supplies us with all things to enjoy. Instruct them to do good, to be rich in good works, to be generous and ready to share, storing up for themselves the treasure of a good foundation for the future, so that they may take hold of that which is life indeed.
I TIMOTHY 6:17-19

Do not store up for yourselves treasures on earth, where moth and rust destroy, and where thieves break in and steal. But store up for yourselves treasures in heaven, where neither moth nor rust destroys, and where thieves do not break in or steal; for where your treasure is, there your heart will be also.
MATTHEW 6:19-21

Therefore be patient, brethren, until the coming of the Lord. The farmer waits for the precious produce of the soil, being patient about it, until it gets the early and late rains. You too be patient; strengthen your hearts, for the coming of the Lord is near.
JAMES 5:7-8

Behold, I am coming quickly, and My reward is with Me, to render to every man according to what he has done.
REVELATION 22:12

And He also went on to say to the one who had invited Him, "When you give a luncheon or a dinner, do not invite your friends or your brothers or your relatives or rich neighbors, otherwise they may also invite you in return and that will be your repayment. But when you give a reception, invite the poor, the crippled, the lame, the blind, and you will be blessed, since they do not have the means to repay you; for you will be repaid at the resurrection of the righteous.
LUKE 14:12-14

LIVE IT OUT

Many people rent storage units around town. Storage is where you accumulate things you want to keep. You accumulate things your house can't hold, and things you can't use right now, and you place them in storage until the time comes that you want or need them. A bank is another example of storage. We put money in the bank or into investments, and we seek to accumulate it. We do that with the future in mind. We expect to need more money for the kids' education or for a new house, or vacations. We know we don't need it now, but there will be a time when we do.

Doing good works is for the sake of someone else now. But a time is coming when we'll need something to work back for us.

And you can't withdraw from an account with nothing in it. You can't go to your storage unit and remove something that has not been stored. In other words, the only thing you can withdraw is what has been deposited and the interest paid on it. The Bible tells the rich to be rich in good works because, in doing those good works, they are building up storage for themselves. God wants to give you back what you've stored up. But if you haven't stored up anything in good works, then there will be nothing to withdraw.

One of the reasons a lot of people are not experiencing more of God is that their storage is empty. They have only been concerned about what they have done and accumulated for themselves, and not the good works that have been transferred from them. Therefore, their storage is empty. You see, God says that you must be future-oriented. When you do good works, you are storing up treasure in heaven and filling an account that will be drawn on when you yourself are in need of it.

REFLECTIONS

1 Do you have a storage unit, garage, basement, or attic where you keep things you don't need right now? What is there, and for what purpose are you saving it?

2 Is it more gratifying to you to see a result immediately or to know that one is coming?

Write about one thing you paid for and received right away. Now write about another thing you've done that will lead to a reward for you at a future time. Which thing are you more excited about?

Do you know someone who has a tendency to pay into their heavenly storage a lot? Describe what you see in them.

"DOING GOOD WORKS IS FOR THE SAKE OF SOMEONE ELSE NOW. BUT A TIME IS COMING WHEN WE'LL NEED SOMETHING TO WORK BACK FOR US.

CHALLENGE

It has been said that what you are recognized and rewarded for on earth is for your encouragement now, and what you are not recognized for will be your reward in heaven. Do you agree? For example, you might spend a Saturday morning cleaning the house, and your spouse and kids notice how fresh everything looks and smells. That's for now! Then you might participate in a project at work where your contribution is ignored or attributed to someone else. That's for later!

Make it a goal to not be acknowledged. You might provide information for someone's presentation, polish your spouse's shoes, pay for someone's coffee, or slip a gift card into someone's pocket. Work with God to notice ways you can share His love. If the recipient attributes your kindness to God's goodness, then you have deposited into your heavenly storage. Even if they don't, and God sees, He will still reward your kindness. But if you ask for applause, then that reward is for here and now only.

He who steals must steal no longer;
but rather he must labor, performing
with his own hands what is good,
so that he will have something to
share with one who has need.
EPHESIANS 4:28

So is the man who stores up treasure for
himself, and is not rich toward God.
LUKE 12:21

Let us not lose heart in doing
good, for in due time we will reap
if we do not grow weary.
GALATIANS 6:9

Love your enemies, and do good, and
lend, expecting nothing in return; and
your reward will be great, and you will
be sons of the Most High; for He Himself
is kind to ungrateful and evil men.
LUKE 6:35

Tabitha's Miracle

Now in Joppa there was a disciple named Tabitha (which translated in Greek is called Dorcas); this woman was abounding with deeds of kindness and charity which she continually did. And it happened at that time that she fell sick and died; and when they had washed her body, they laid it in an upper room. Since Lydda was near Joppa, the disciples, having heard that Peter was there, sent two men to him, imploring him, "Do not delay in coming to us." So Peter arose and went with them. When he arrived, they brought him into the upper room; and all the widows stood beside him, weeping and showing all the tunics and garments that Dorcas used to make while she was with them. But Peter sent them all out and knelt down and prayed, and turning to the body, he said, "Tabitha, arise." And she opened her eyes, and when she saw Peter, she sat up. And he gave her his hand and raised her up; and calling the saints and widows, he presented her alive. It became known all over Joppa, and many believed in the Lord.

ACTS 9:36-42

How blessed is the man who does not walk in the counsel of the wicked,
Nor stand in the path of sinners,
Nor sit in the seat of scoffers!
But his delight is in the law of the Lord,
And in His law he meditates
day and night.
He will be like a tree firmly
planted by streams of water,
Which yields its fruit in its season
And its leaf does not wither;
And in whatever he does, he prospers.

PSALM 1:1-3

LIVE IT OUT

Don't spend your life climbing the ladder of success, and when you get to the top, find out it's leaning against the wrong wall.

Instead, climb like Tabitha.

In the house of Joppa, there was a disciple named Tabitha. She was a woman abounding with deeds of kindness and charity. She was rich with good works, regularly helping somebody out in a responsible way. But she fell sick and died. When the disciples with her heard that Peter was there in the next town over, in Lydda, they sent a couple of guys to him, begging him to come to Tabitha's house. So Peter went with them. When he arrived, they brought him into the upper room where all the widows were weeping and mourning. They showed Peter all of the tunics and garments that Tabitha used to make while she was with them. In other words, these mourners were the women that Tabitha had helped.

Peter saw the good that Tabitha had done while she was alive. So he sent everyone out of the room, then he knelt and prayed. Then he told her to get up. She opened her eyes. When she saw Peter, she sat up. And he gave her his hand, helped her stand, and presented her alive to the saints and widows mourning her death.

Tabitha got a miracle. But before she needed a miracle, the Bible describes her character. She was abounding in good works. She used her skill as a tunic maker to clothe widows. And when she died, her presence and her good works were incredibly missed. So Peter was able to come and resurrect her.

The point is this: When you do good works for God's glory, and you come to an issue your own attempts or good works can't fix—like Tabitha's tunics couldn't fix her illness—look to God. Like Nehemiah, pray "Remember me for good." God may have a reason to allow the issue to continue. That's where trust comes in. But if He doesn't, look to Him to respond.

God can raise you up out of your situation. God can raise you up out of your crisis. But as your blessing rises, make sure your good works are rising with them. As your resources rise, make sure your sensitivity rises with them. Make sure that when your need comes, you have God's full attention.

REFLECTIONS

What gifts or talents has God given specifically to you?

How do you use them? Is it for profit or personal gain only, or do you share them with others at no cost? Or is it a mix of those?

How have you used whatever success or gain you have received?

Write about a time that you needed a big miracle and received it. Now write about a time you needed a big miracle and didn't receive it. Have you asked God why you received one miracle but not the other?

“DON’T SPEND YOUR LIFE CLIMBING THE LADDER OF SUCCESS, AND WHEN YOU GET TO THE TOP, FIND OUT IT’S LEANING AGAINST THE WRONG WALL.

CHALLENGE

Romans 4:4 says that we should be paid fairly for the work that we do. And yet we are also called to do good works for no earthly reward. On the surface, this can seem like conflicting evidence. But we know that the resources of heaven are limitless and that as God's children we have access to His kingdom. So when we give, it will be with a mix of sacrifice (giving up something valuable to us) and abundance (trusting that with God, there is always more).

Consider what you have to offer based on your skills and talents. What unique ability can you share with those in need? Tabitha sewed clothes. Mary and Martha, along with their brother Lazarus, had a home big enough to host and serve many people. You have unique offerings that matter. You may use them to make a wage, and you can also use them to benefit those who cannot pay. Be assured that every time you serve others in love, your wage goes into your heavenly bank account.

Do not withhold good from
those to whom it is due,
When it is in your power to do it.
Do not say to your neighbor,
"Go, and come back,
And tomorrow I will give it,"
When you have it with you.
PROVERBS 3:27-28

Whatever you do, do your work heartily,
as for the Lord rather than for men,
knowing that from the Lord you will
receive the reward of the inheritance.
It is the Lord Christ whom you serve.
COLOSSIANS 3:23-24

Do not work for the food which
perishes, but for the food which
endures to eternal life, which the Son
of Man will give to you, for on Him
the Father, God, has set His seal.
JOHN 6:27

Therefore, my beloved brethren, be
steadfast, immovable, always abounding
in the work of the Lord, knowing that
your toil is not in vain in the Lord.
I CORINTHIANS 15:58

DAY 05

The Effects of the Son

If you abide in Me, and My words abide in you, ask whatever you wish, and it will be done for you.
JOHN 15:7

Abide in Me, and I in you. As the branch cannot bear fruit of itself unless it abides in the vine, so neither can you unless you abide in Me.
JOHN 15:4

For we are a fragrance of Christ to God among those who are being saved and among those who are perishing.
II CORINTHIANS 2:15

And walk in love, just as Christ also loved you and gave Himself up for us, an offering and a sacrifice to God as a fragrant aroma.
EPHESIANS 5:2

One who is gracious to a poor
man lends to the Lord,
And He will repay him for his good deed.
PROVERBS 19:17

He who loves money will not be satisfied with money, nor he who loves abundance with its income. This too is futility.
ECCLESIASTES 5:10

But remember the Lord your God, for it is He who gives you the ability to produce wealth, and so confirms His covenant, which He swore to your ancestors, as it is today.
DEUTERONOMY 8:18 NIV

And if anyone gives even a cup of cold water to one of these little ones who is My disciple, truly I tell you, that person will certainly not lose their reward.
MATTHEW 10:42 NIV

Trust in the Lord with all your heart
And do not lean on your
own understanding.
In all your ways acknowledge Him,
And He will make your paths straight.
PROVERBS 3:5-6

LIVE IT OUT

In most places the summertime is when it gets hot. And when it gets hot, a lot of people enjoy spending time outside in the sun. While you're out there, it will become evident that you've spent a lot of time in the sun. You'll feel the heat. You'll fan yourself. You'll sweat. And if you spend too much time in it, you're going to smell! In other words, it will become evident that the sun has affected you. Many will wish not to be affected in any extended amount of time by the sun, so they're going to get out of it as quickly as possible because they like to be cool.

In a similar way, it will also be very clear when the SON has affected you. When the Son has affected you, it's going to show up in the way you touch the lives of others. If you do not touch the lives of others, then you've not been affected by the Son. No matter how many church services you go to, no matter how much praise you do, no matter how much waving of your hands in the air, no matter how many pews you flip, if lives are not benefited from the time you've spent in the Son, then it's because He has not yet rubbed off on you.

The longer you're in the Son, the more sensitive you are to others. The less time you spend in the Son, the less sensitive you are to others.

Jesus wants you to know that the way you know you tangibly love Him is that you're touching the lives of others. If others' lives go untouched, your love for Him is low.

A lot of us do the Son like we do the sun. We don't want to hang out too long. Because if we do, we might love people we don't want to love or help people we don't want to help. We might forgive people we don't want to forgive and lift up people we'd rather hold down. In the Son, we might sweat love.

REFLECTIONS

In what ways has your life been touched by others who have spent time in the Son?

Describe a season of your life when you experienced a greater sense of productivity in His love.

Describe a desert season, or a time when you didn't feel as close to His love.

Are you more comfortable in the Son, with all of its effects, or in the spiritual shade? Why?

What would you like to see changed in the way you pursue time with Jesus?

"

THE LONGER YOU'RE IN THE SON, THE MORE SENSITIVE YOU ARE TO OTHERS. THE LESS TIME YOU SPEND IN THE SON, THE LESS SENSITIVE YOU ARE TO OTHERS.

CHALLENGE

Any physics professor will tell you that *for every action there is an equal and opposite reaction*. In other words, you can't push on something and expect it not to push back. Your influence, whether good or bad, will affect the recipient. And every moment you spend seeking the Lord will benefit you, the kingdom of heaven, and the world around you. Time with God will never yield nothing. It can't because your action to seek Him will stir up His attention and reaction of love.

Your challenge today is simple: Sit with Jesus. Find a quiet place to be with Him. Leave your phone at home and bring a paper Bible. Even ten minutes will strengthen your spirit. And ten minutes a day for a week will build longevity. As you learn to sit with Him, listening for His voice and placing no expectations on what He wants to say, your time with Him will flow out through your interactions with others. Ask God to speak through you to bless someone else. And enjoy your time in the Son.

And He also went on to say to the one who had invited Him, "When you give a luncheon or a dinner, do not invite your friends or your brothers or your relatives or rich neighbors, otherwise they may also invite you in return and that will be your repayment. But when you give a reception, invite the poor, the crippled, the lame, the blind, and you will be blessed, since they do not have the means to repay you; for you will be repaid at the resurrection of the righteous."

LUKE 14:12-14

On the first day of every week each one of you is to put aside and save, as he may prosper, so that no collections be made when I come.

I CORINTHIANS 16:2

By this we know that we are in Him: the one who says he abides in Him ought himself to walk in the same manner as He walked.

I JOHN 2:5-6

The one who says he is in the Light and yet hates his brother is in the darkness until now. The one who loves his brother abides in the Light and there is no cause for stumbling in him.

I JOHN 2:9-10

The Useful Gift

But when the Son of Man comes in His glory, and all the angels with Him, then He will sit on His glorious throne. All the nations will be gathered before Him; and He will separate them from one another, as the shepherd separates the sheep from the goats; and He will put the sheep on His right, and the goats on the left.

Then the King will say to those on His right, "Come, you who are blessed of My Father, inherit the kingdom prepared for you from the foundation of the world. For I was hungry, and you gave Me something to eat; I was thirsty, and you gave Me something to drink; I was a stranger, and you invited Me in; naked, and you clothed Me; I was sick, and you visited Me; I was in prison, and you came to Me." Then the righteous will answer Him, "Lord, when did we see You hungry, and feed You, or thirsty, and give You something to drink? And when did we see You a stranger, and invite You in, or naked, and clothe You? When did we see You sick, or in prison, and come to You?" The King will answer and say to them, "Truly I say to you, to the extent that you did it to one of these brothers of Mine, even the least of them, you did it to Me."
MATTHEW 25:31-40

Jesus called them to Himself and said, "You know that the rulers of the Gentiles lord it over them, and their great men exercise authority over them. It is not this way among you, but whoever wishes to become great among you shall be your servant, and whoever wishes to be first among you shall be your slave; just as the Son of Man did not come to be served, but to serve, and to give His life a ransom for many.
MATTHEW 20:25-28

LIVE IT OUT

Have you ever had someone buy you something on your birthday that you did not want, did not ask for, and could not use? It became a wasted gift. You put it in the attic or threw it in the trash, or worse yet, you gave it to somebody else on their birthday! The item was useless to you.

Unfortunately, a lot of people give Jesus stuff He can't use. They give Him something He doesn't want, but they feel they have to do something so they give Him anything. What Jesus says He wants is for us to touch the life of another in His name. He wants us to affect those who can't help us back. Those people who can do nothing in return—they're without clothes or food, they're thirsty, in prison, helpless. We live in a world of *quid pro quo*, this for that. There's nothing wrong with cutting a deal if it's a legitimate deal. That's what business is all about. But Jesus wants to know that your relationship with Him is not business. He says, "If you know Me, and if you spend time with Me, then I'll be pouring out from you, burning in and through you, and it will touch others."

At the time of judgment, Matthew 25 tells us, Jesus will say that the way He knows we served Him is by how we served others.

Jesus says, *You want to know what to get Me as a present? Give me the love you say you have for Me, and transfer it. Touch the lives of .others.* There is a direct correlation between ministry and love for God, and ministry and love for others. It's a love that doesn't ask for anything back. It's a love that, in fact, touches those who couldn't offer anything in return if they wanted to. The more God sees you do this, the more blessed you will be in the Son.

REFLECTIONS

1 Name a time you received a gift you couldn't use. What did you do with it?

2 Do you feel obligated to serve God? To complete tasks for Him? If so, how does that generally play out?

Describe a time when you witnessed or were a part of the love of Jesus touching someone in just the right way.

Name one or two current needs that you can't fill yourself. Write a prayer asking God to help you fill the needs.

“

AT THE TIME OF JUDGMENT, MATTHEW 25 TELLS US, JESUS WILL SAY THAT THE WAY HE KNOWS WE SERVED HIM IS BY HOW WE SERVED OTHERS.

CHALLENGE

Consider how you go about finding gifts for the people you love. You might think about their current interests, something you know they don't have, or something they have that needs to be replaced. You might see an item in a store that reminds you of them. You might make something yourself, sharing your time and talent to create something meaningful. At any rate, buying gifts for those you love is rarely a quick jaunt to the store to pick up the first item you see. And what would be a true gift for one person might be a trash treasure for another.

The gifts that Jesus loves to receive actually go to another person first. And one great way to offer a one-way gift is by writing a letter. Think of someone you can write to, telling them how you feel about them, or simply filling their mailbox with a non-junk mail envelope, a handwritten address, and a silly card inside. Make it a point to make someone's day, and purpose not to expect a "thank you" in return. Know that when you build others up, you are blessing God's heart.

Then they themselves also will answer, "Lord, when did we see You hungry, or thirsty, or a stranger, or naked, or sick, or in prison, and did not take care of You?" Then He will answer them, "Truly I say to you, to the extent that you did not do it to one of the least of these, you did not do it to Me."

MATTHEW 25:44-45

Everyone should look not to his own interests, but rather to the interests of others.

PHILIPPIANS 2:4 CSB

We know love by this, that He laid down His life for us; and we ought to lay down our lives for the brethren.

I JOHN 3:16

A generous person will prosper; whoever refreshes others will be refreshed.

PROVERBS 11:25 NIV

DAY 07

Not Home Yet

But a Samaritan, who was on a journey, came upon him; and when he saw him, he felt compassion, and came to him and bandaged up his wounds, pouring oil and wine on them; and he put him on his own beast, and brought him to an inn and took care of him. On the next day he took out two denarii and gave them to the innkeeper and said, "Take care of him; and whatever more you spend, when I return I will repay you."
LUKE 10:33-35

But when you give to the poor, do not let your left hand know what your right hand is doing, so that your giving will be in secret; and your Father who sees what is done in secret will reward you.
MATTHEW 6:3-4

For the Son of Man is going to come in the glory of His Father with His angels, and will then repay every man according to his deeds.
MATTHEW 16:27

In My Father's house are many dwelling places; if it were not so, I would have told you; for I go to prepare a place for you. If I go and prepare a place for you, I will come again and receive you to Myself, that where I am, there you may be also.
JOHN 14:2-3

LIVE IT OUT

Henry Morrison was a missionary to Africa. He had spent many years there and was on his way back home to the United States to retire. The president of the United States was also on Henry's boat. And when the boat sailed into the harbor, there were throngs of people waiting to welcome the president back. Hundreds and hundreds! Bands were playing and people were celebrating to see the return of the president with his entourage.

One of the last passengers to disembark was Henry Morrison. As he got off the boat, there were tears in his eyes. No one was there to welcome him home. There was no band, no group of people excited to see him and congratulate him on serving the Lord faithfully for so many years.

Suddenly, the Holy Spirit hit him with an epiphany. In his mind's eye, Henry imagined himself at the Pearly Gates. Saint Peter was there to welcome him, and when Peter opened the door, there were thousands of people applauding him whose lives he had touched all those years in Africa. They chanted his name—Henry! Henry! Henry! And at that moment, he imagined a voice from the back of the throng—God's voice—saying, "Henry, you're not home yet."

You may not get all the applause you deserve right now, but if you touch lives for good, in His name, He records it and adds it to the accolades for your coming home party.

God wants you to know that you have not wasted time, energy, effort, or resources when His definition of good works is being expressed through your ministry, whether formally or informally, as God leads you in different scenarios of life. When those people who can't pay you back are touched by your life, there will be a repayment. But if you demand repayment or recognition now, He says, you will have already been paid. So expect and demand nothing, knowing there's going to be a whopper of a payday!

REFLECTIONS

How do you feel about being recognized or applauded?

How do you feel when someone else is recognized or applauded and you are not?

Is it normal, in your daily life, for people to see you at work? Or is your work more invisible?

4 Do you find more satisfaction in doing things for those you love or for those whom God sets in your path seemingly randomly?

5 How open are you to serving those you don't know, don't see, or don't like?

"

YOU MAY NOT GET ALL THE APPLAUSE YOU DESERVE RIGHT NOW, BUT IF YOU TOUCH LIVES FOR GOOD, IN HIS NAME, HE RECORDS IT AND ADDS IT TO THE ACCOLADES FOR YOUR COMING HOME PARTY.

CHALLENGE

There's nothing wrong with having your friends over for a party. But God would say, don't have your friends and family over and expect a reward from that later. It's not rewardable, because that's your comfort crew, and they can help you or invite you right back. In fact, you get ticked if they don't invite you to their party! The kind of reward God gives is for those who invite people who can't even have a party to invite you back to. God rewards kindness to the blind, lame, and outcast—not in an irresponsible way but for those who are in a condition they can't fix.

Find one person or organization that fits those qualifications, such as a nursing home or foster home. Do one thing to go out of your way for a person in need. There are some people in another country who throw dinner parties for prostitutes, give them makeovers and mirrors, and tell them they are beautiful, valuable, and seen. Find your way to raise up someone who believes they are too low to be cared about. And know that your achievement will be celebrated loudly in heaven.

Bear one another's burdens, and
thereby fulfill the law of Christ.
GALATIANS 6:2

Do not neglect doing good and sharing,
for with such sacrifices God is pleased.
HEBREWS 13:16

One who is gracious to a poor
man lends to the Lord,
And He will repay him for his good deed.
PROVERBS 19:17

When God's people are in need,
be ready to help them. Always be
eager to practice hospitality.
ROMANS 12:13 NLT

Do not withhold good from
those to whom it is due,
When it is in your power to do it.
PROVERBS 3:27

A Special Purpose

As He passed by, He saw a man blind from birth. And His disciples asked Him, "Rabbi, who sinned, this man or his parents, that he would be born blind?" Jesus answered, "It was neither that this man sinned, nor his parents; but it was so that the works of God might be displayed in him. We must work the works of Him who sent Me as long as it is day; night is coming when no one can work. While I am in the world, I am the Light of the world." When He had said this, He spat on the ground, and made clay of the spittle, and applied the clay to his eyes, and said to him, "Go, wash In the pool of Siloam" (which is translated, Sent). So he went away and washed, and came back seeing. Therefore the neighbors, and those who previously saw him as a beggar, were saying, "Is not this the one who used to sit and beg?" Others were saying, "This is he," still others were saying, "No, but he is like him." He kept saying, "I am the one." So they were saying to him, "How then were your eyes opened?" He answered, "The man who is called Jesus made clay, and anointed my eyes, and said to me, 'Go to Siloam and wash'; so I went away and washed, and I received sight."

JOHN 9:1-11

They came to Bethsaida. And they brought a blind man to Jesus and implored Him to touch him. Taking the blind man by the hand, He brought him out of the village; and after spitting on his eyes and laying His hands on him, He asked him, "Do you see anything?" And he looked up and said, "I see men, for I see them like trees, walking around." Then again He laid His hands on his eyes; and he looked intently and was restored, and began to see everything clearly.

MARK 8:22-25

LIVE IT OUT

When Jesus encountered a young man who was blind, He contradicted the common belief of the day that the man or his parents had sinned in order to cause his blindness. Instead, he said, "it was so that the works of God might be displayed in him." In other words, Jesus said, the man was blind because God had a plan for him! And all of a sudden, the kid with special needs was *really* special. Because even though he was born with a challenge, Jesus assured the man that he was born with a challenge *and* a purpose.

We all struggle with something. While some of us have impairments that are more noticeable than others, we all have weaknesses. The good news is that God's power is made perfect in our weakness (II Corinthians 12). So the next time you run across somebody who can't see, or whose mental capacity isn't where yours is, don't look down on them. Instead, focus on your struggle and your purpose. Because people's apparent weaknesses are often there for a divine reason and a divine purpose.

Jesus did something very unusual for the blind young man: He spit into the dirt. He took the dirt in his hand, spit into it, and mixed it together into a sort of clay. He applied the clay to the young man's eyes and sent him to wash his eyes off in the pool of Siloam.

This is a message for people who are ready to see, using the blind man. All of his life, this young man had a special need for this special moment. In order for Jesus to spit, He had to project it forward out of His mouth. He spit in the dirt. God created man from the dirt, so something coming out of Jesus' mouth mixed with what He made man out of. It's the voice of God mixing with the humanity of man. The Word of God and the dirt of man being comingled.

Then He told the young man to go and wash at a particular place. When he did, he began to see things he had never seen before.

If you will ever let God's Word touch your humanity to such a degree that you do what He says, then you can experience a miracle in your life.

God has things He wants to show you, places He wants to lead you, and situations He wants to guide you in. When you allow His Word to unblind you, it will change your perspective and your entire life.

REFLECTIONS

1. What is your experience with people who have special needs?

2. Describe a time you witnessed God use someone who would likely be considered different from others.

3. Describe a time God was glorified through your struggles.

4 What unique challenges are you facing today? Do you think they can serve a kingdom purpose? How?

5 How has your perspective changed since you allowed God's Word to touch you?

"

IF YOU WILL EVER LET GOD'S WORD TOUCH YOUR HUMANITY TO SUCH A DEGREE THAT YOU DO WHAT HE SAYS, THEN YOU CAN EXPERIENCE A MIRACLE IN YOUR LIFE.

CHALLENGE

Joni Eareckson Tada had a diving accident when she was a teenager and has been paralyzed for over sixty years. Churches all over the world use her materials, as God allowed a negative to produce a positive for His kingdom. One day He will explain His rationale to her. But in the meantime, people around the world with injuries or defects are being ministered to because Joni has ignited churches to not forget those who are hurting. She has said, "If I could turn back the hands of time, and not go to that lake, not do that dive and swim into that pool—I wouldn't do it. Because my experience with God has been so rich and my ministry impact so great. God has used a mess and allowed me to minister with a miracle."

What has had such a negative impact on your life that perhaps God is choosing to use it for good? If you pray in thanks and surrender, that will open the doors to whatever purpose He has for your challenge.

His master said to him, "Well done, good and faithful slave. You were faithful with a few things, I will put you in charge of many things; enter into the joy of your master."

MATTHEW 25:23

Whoever in the name of a disciple gives to one of these little ones even a cup of cold water to drink, truly I say to you, he shall not lose his reward.

MATTHEW 10:42

Jesus said, "For judgment I came into this world, so that those who do not see may see, and that those who see may become blind."

JOHN 9:39

The Lord opens the eyes of the blind;
The Lord raises up those
who are bowed down;
The Lord loves the righteous.

PSALM 146:8

DAY 09

Your Neighbor

Jesus replied and said, "A man was going down from Jerusalem to Jericho, and fell among robbers, and they stripped him and beat him, and went away leaving him half dead. And by chance a priest was going down on that road, and when he saw him, he passed by on the other side. Likewise a Levite also, when he came to the place and saw him, passed by on the other side. But a Samaritan, who was on a journey, came upon him; and when he saw him, he felt compassion, and came to him and bandaged up his wounds, pouring oil and wine on them; and he put him on his own beast, and brought him to an inn and took care of him. On the next day he took out two denarii and gave them to the innkeeper and said, 'Take care of him; and whatever more you spend, when I return I will repay you.' Which of these three do you think proved to be a neighbor to the man who fell into the robbers' hands?" And he said, "The one who showed mercy toward him." Then Jesus said to him, "Go and do the same."
LUKE 10:30-35

Therefore the Samaritan woman said to Him, "How is it that You, being a Jew, ask me for a drink since I am a Samaritan woman?" (For Jews have no dealings with Samaritans.) Jesus answered and said to her, "If you knew the gift of God, and who it is who says to you, 'Give Me a drink,' you would have asked Him, and He would have given you living water."
JOHN 4:9-10

LIVE IT OUT

You might know the story of the man who was walking from Jerusalem to Jericho when he was attacked, robbed, and beaten until he was half dead. The story tells of three men who passed him on the road: a priest, a Levite, and a Samaritan. The former two were fellow Jews to the man who was beaten. The latter was a rival. But only the Samaritan stopped to help.

Now, the priest and the Levite, in theory, were good churchgoing people. We're not talking about sinners; we're talking about servants of the living God. But when they encountered a fellow man in trouble, they crossed to the other side of the road and walked on by. Maybe they were afraid of also becoming victims. Maybe they were late for Sunday dinner. Maybe they didn't want to touch a dead body, as it would have contaminated them according to the Law. At any rate, they moved along and left the man half dead on the side of the road.

The Samaritan was also on a journey, with someplace to go. But the story says that he felt compassion. He came to the man, bandaged his wounds, and carried him to an inn to be looked after. He paid the medical bill and promised to return if the bill was higher than the two denarii he had with him.

Jesus told the story of the Good Samaritan to a lawyer who had asked who his neighbor was because Jesus had said that loving our neighbor is like loving God with everything we have and are. This story was a curveball because a priest or a Levite would be a brother to that Jewish lawyer, but a Samaritan would be an enemy. Yet the Samaritan was the one who felt compassion on the man and did something.

Your neighbor is the person whose need you see, whose need you feel, and whose need you address.

Pay close attention to those situations for which you feel compassion. Consider whether you have the resources to address that need. It may be the very neighbor that God is highlighting for you to serve in His name and for His glory.

REFLECTIONS

Make a list of some people who would appear to be your "natural" neighbors.

Make a list of people whose needs you often feel compassion for.

Describe a time when you helped someone "beyond reason." How did it turn out?

Describe a time when you were helped "beyond reason" by someone else. How did that go?

“YOUR NEIGHBOR IS THE PERSON WHOSE NEED YOU SEE, WHOSE NEED YOU FEEL, AND WHOSE NEED YOU ADDRESS.

CHALLENGE

There are thousands of needs out there. You see them all but you don't feel them all the same. You drive by most of them, but some of them grab you. Some you feel but can't do anything about. And in other cases you see it, feel it, and are able to do something about it. When you are able to show mercy to someone who needs mercy, that is the time to act in a neighborly way.

If a person or situation has come to mind in the last few minutes, step out of your way this week to help them. If not, then ask God to reveal a situation that you are tailor-made to see, feel, and do something about. The Samaritan wasn't out looking for a service project. But he was available and open to what he encountered. Open your heart to God's ideas, release any fear you may have about getting uncomfortable, and watch what He wants to do in and through you.

But the tax collector, standing some
distance away, was even unwilling
to lift up his eyes to heaven, but was
beating his breast, saying, "God,
be merciful to me, the sinner!"

LUKE 18:13

The merciful man does himself good,
But the cruel man does himself harm.

PROVERBS 11:17

But You, O Lord, are a God
merciful and gracious,
Slow to anger and abundant in
lovingkindness and truth.

PSALM 86:15

Then they themselves also will answer,
"Lord, when did we see You hungry,
or thirsty, or a stranger, or naked, or
sick, or in prison, and did not take care
of You?" Then He will answer them,
"Truly I say to you, to the extent that
you did not do it to one of the least
of these, you did not do it to Me."

MATTHEW 25:44-45

Serving Eye to Eye

Therefore, I exhort the elders among you, as your fellow elder and witness of the sufferings of Christ, and a partaker also of the glory that is to be revealed, shepherd the flock of God among you, exercising oversight not under compulsion, but voluntarily, according to the will of God; and not for sordid gain, but with eagerness; nor yet as lording it over those allotted to your charge, but proving to be examples to the flock.
I PETER 5:1-3

All of you, clothe yourselves with humility toward one another, for God is opposed to the proud, but gives grace to the humble. Therefore humble yourselves under the mighty hand of God, that He may exalt you at the proper time, casting all your anxiety on Him, because He cares for you.
I PETER 5:5-7

In everything I showed you that by working hard in this manner you must help the weak and remember the words of the Lord Jesus, that He Himself said, "It is more blessed to give than to receive."
ACTS 20:35

For the poor will never cease to be in the land; therefore I command you, saying, "You shall freely open your hand to your brother, to your needy and poor in your land."
DEUTERONOMY 15:11

LIVE IT OUT

A group of students were told to preach a sermon on Luke 10 for their final project. The students worked hard getting their sermons together for their Good Samaritan presentations. As they arrived for their ten o'clock class that morning, there was a broken, beaten, raggedy, dirty, smelly guy sitting outside the door with a little bucket. The students noticed but went in so as not to be late for their class.

Each student waxed eloquently for twenty minutes apiece. Their sermons were awe-inspiring and well-researched. But when they had all finished, the professor stood at the front of the class and said, "You have all failed. You preached a great sermon, each of you. But you ignored your neighbor out there on your way in. I asked that man to come and sit outside our class because I wanted to see who could preach and live it out, not just preach about it."

Neighbors are not projects. They're not just places you send money, people you need to deliver, or projects you need to manage. In 1965 the great society program was passed. It was well-intentioned, but it created a mess of problems that are reverberating today. If I live in Dallas, it's not going to be someone in Washington who fixes my pain. I need somebody who sees me. I need somebody who feels my pain, who passes me on the stoop and looks me in the eyes to see that I am a person with a problem in need of a biblical solution.

God is not against your progress if done biblically, spiritually, and legitimately. He is against progress that makes you think, feel, or act like you're better than others who are not where you are. God wants you to reach neighbors, and He will put neighbors in front of you. He will bring people whom you see, who dig into your heart, and whom you can't shake.

Don't be satisfied to write a check because God wants life to touch lives and people to touch people.

REFLECTIONS

1 What do you think the students were thinking when they passed the homeless man on the way to their class?

2 How could they have handled the situation differently?

3 How does a person's progress threaten their perspective on those who are in lower positions, or who need help?

4 How can somebody keep themselves humble and open to God at work?

5 How have you changed as you have progressed in life?

“

DON'T BE SATISFIED TO WRITE A CHECK BECAUSE GOD WANTS LIFE TO TOUCH LIVES AND PEOPLE TO TOUCH PEOPLE.

CHALLENGE

Progressing in life is not a bad thing if it is in line with kingdom principles. But as you progress, it's important to keep tabs on how your perspective is changing, how the world is changing around you, and how you can use your current station in life to serve others. The Bible is full of reminders for older women and men to mentor and care for younger women and men. No matter where you are in life, you have more experience and wisdom than someone else down the line.

Likewise, if you have a car, you may find someone who needs a ride. If you have a house, you may find a small group that needs a place to meet. If you have twenty dollars, you may find someone who needs a meal. The need is out there, and our attitude about finding it says so much about our character. Find an unconventional way to offer what you have to someone who is now where you once were. Whether it's time, talent, or resources, you are well off compared to someone else who isn't as far along. Certainly, God will notice you reaching back to lift someone up.

Do not sharply rebuke an older man, but rather appeal to him as a father, to the younger men as brothers, the older women as mothers, and the younger women as sisters, in all purity.

I TIMOTHY 5:1-2

Give, and it will be given to you. They will pour into your lap a good measure—pressed down, shaken together, and running over. For by your standard of measure it will be measured to you in return. He also spoke a parable to them: "A blind man cannot guide a blind man, can he? Will they not both fall into a pit? A pupil is not above his teacher; but everyone, after he has been fully trained, will be like his teacher."

LUKE 6:38-40

And do not neglect doing good and sharing, for with such sacrifices God is pleased.

HEBREWS 13:16

DAY 11

Peacemakers

Blessed are the peacemakers, for they shall be called sons of God.
MATTHEW 5:9

If possible, so far as it depends on you, be at peace with all men.
ROMANS 12:18

Salt is good; but if the salt becomes unsalty, with what will you make it salty again? Have salt in yourselves, and be at peace with one another.
MARK 9:50

This is the message we have heard from Him and announce to you, that God is Light, and in Him there is no darkness at all.
I JOHN 1:5

Love is patient, love is kind. It does not envy, it does not boast, it is not proud. It does not dishonor others, it is not self-seeking, it is not easily angered, it keeps no record of wrongs.
I CORINTHIANS 13:4-5 NIV

Greater love has no one than this, that one lay down his life for his friends.
JOHN 15:13

Always be humble and gentle. Be patient with each other, making allowance for each other's faults because of your love.
EPHESIANS 4:2 NLT

Now may the God of peace Himself sanctify you entirely; and may your spirit and soul and body be preserved complete, without blame at the coming of our Lord Jesus Christ.
I THESSALONIANS 5:23

LIVE IT OUT

In 1945 the United Nations was established with one of its primary goals being to maintain global peace. At that time, there was a feeling that we needed something to help orchestrate peace around the world. War is so natural to the human condition. The United Nations sends peacekeeping forces to help mediate and mitigate conflicts that occur between nations.

Peace is hard to come by. In the nearly four thousand years of recorded human history, there have been only 268 years where there was no war. War is normal, not only for nations but for many of us. We battle our own internal conflicts, and that is war. There are domestic wars between couples who seem not to have been married by a justice of the peace but by the secretary of war! There are conflicts between parents and children, coworkers, and of course social, racial, personality, and political wars. It gets you a little worried when peace comes, because you know it won't last long. There is war waiting to happen around every corner.

Yet we find a blessing in Matthew 5:9: "Blessed are the peacemakers, for they shall be called the sons of God." Who are the peacemakers? Peacemakers are people who bring harmony where conflict used to exist. This isn't just not fighting. We know that people can stop arguing but be in a cold silence. That's not peace. No, just because you stop shooting doesn't mean you stop fighting.

To be a peacemaker is to be someone who, rather than running from conflict, faces it with the truth.

He or she does it by exposing and addressing the sin that has led to the conflict, resulting in a right relationship between the combatants.

A peacemaker is more than a peace-keeper. It's more than standing between two people and telling them not to fight, knowing that as soon as you step away it could start again. Peacemaking means resolving the reason for the conflict so that when you step back, the combatants can now get along because there has been a real resolution.

REFLECTIONS

1 Are you a peacemaker, a peacekeeper, or someone who avoids conflict at all costs?

2 Do you know a successful peacemaker? What qualities does this person possess?

3 What happens when two sides refuse to see eye to eye? Can resolution happen?

4 Describe a time when a true resolution came between two combatants—either in yourself, among people, or in the world.

5 What are the risks of peacemaking? Is trying always worth it?

"

TO BE A PEACEMAKER IS TO BE SOMEONE WHO, RATHER THAN RUNNING FROM CONFLICT, FACES IT WITH THE TRUTH.

CHALLENGE

War is a battle where opposing sides see things differently and are willing to defend their perspective. Sometimes that defense happens physically, and sometimes it happens internally with an unwillingness to budge on a thought or view. Any war is destructive because it hinders unity, which is what we are called to in Christ.

Peacemaking is an art. It requires prayer, patience, creativity, strategy, and courage. This week, take one "war" before God and ask Him for all of the above. Take one step toward helping two parties find peace between them. This might mean meeting with each party and assessing the problem from each viewpoint. Or maybe you understand the problem, and it's time to act on behalf of truth. You may be the perfect mediator, or you may be the one to line up the perfect mediator. Any step you take in the direction of resolution, hope, and unity for His glory is a good one. And remember, God desires peace too. So you will not be acting alone. He will be right alongside you.

He is before all things, and in
Him all things hold together.
COLOSSIANS 1:17 NIV

Therefore I, the prisoner of the Lord,
implore you to walk in a manner
worthy of the calling with which you
have been called, with all humility and
gentleness, with patience, showing
tolerance for one another in love,
being diligent to preserve the unity
of the Spirit in the bond of peace.
EPHESIANS 4:1-3

Beyond all these things put on love,
which is the perfect bond of unity.
Let the peace of Christ rule in your
hearts, to which indeed you were
called in one body; and be thankful.
COLOSSIANS 3:14-15

DAY 12

Access

But now in Christ Jesus you who formerly were far off have been brought near by the blood of Christ. For He Himself is our peace, who made both groups into one and broke down the barrier of the dividing wall, by abolishing in His flesh the enmity, which is the Law of commandments contained in ordinances, so that in Himself He might make the two into one new man, thus establishing peace, and might reconcile them both in one body to God through the cross, by it having put to death the enmity. And He came and preached peace to you who were far away, and peace to those who were near; for through Him we both have our access in one Spirit to the Father. So then you are no longer strangers and aliens, but you are fellow citizens with the saints, and are of God's household, having been built on the foundation of the apostles and prophets, Christ Jesus Himself being the corner stone, in whom the whole building, being fitted together, is growing into a holy temple in the Lord, in whom you also are being built together into a dwelling of God in the Spirit.

EPHESIANS 2:13-22

LIVE IT OUT

There is a true story from the 1800s about a man who sat on a park bench outside of the White House, crying. A little boy came up to him and asked, "What's wrong, sir?" The man told him, "I have this big family issue that only the president could solve. But they won't let me get in to see the president." The little boy held his hand out to the man and said, "Follow me." He walked the man past the gate and past the inner guard. He walked into the Oval Office and said, "This man wants to talk to you, Dad." President Lincoln said, "Thank you, son. Sir, my son brought you here so have a seat." In other words, the father recognized his son and gave him access.

Being a peacemaker is critical to being recognized as God's son or daughter, and being recognized is critical to your access. Answered prayer. Hearing from heaven. Watching God solve problems before you arrive. See, people will call you a son or daughter of God when they see that you have a connection they don't have.

Ephesians 2:13-22 is rich with the beautiful truth about access to God and becoming makers of peace. First, we need Jesus. It was His blood at the cross that allowed us access. Second, He is our peace. And we can't make what we don't have access to. As sons and daughters, we can enjoy the peace that Jesus came to give.

You might ask what all of this has to do with me fighting, with myself, my mate, or my coworkers. And the answer is, everything! The way Jesus gives peace is through the cross. And the cross is a place of judgment. It's a hurtful, painful place of blood. At the cross, you don't say, "Can't we all just get along?" At the cross, sin is being addressed and judged. And because of that judgment, reconciliation happens.

The only reason you and I as Christians have peace with God is because of a nasty, bloody cross.

The suffering of Jesus allows us to have peace with God and with others. Because the blood that judged sin on the cross is the same blood that judges sin today.

If you're going to be a peacemaker, you must be willing to get bloody through the addressing of sin so that the blood of Christ can bring peace.

REFLECTIONS

What does "access to the Father" mean to you?

What makes you comfortable or uncomfortable with the idea of addressing sin in your life? What about helping others address their own sin for the sake of peace?

How does the peace of Jesus differ from earthly peace?

Do you consider yourself a peacemaker? Why or why not?

“

THE ONLY REASON YOU AND I AS CHRISTIANS **HAVE PEACE WITH GOD** IS BECAUSE OF A NASTY, BLOODY CROSS.

CHALLENGE

How familiar are you with the cross of Jesus? Do you spend time at the foot of it? It's important to know what His peace feels like in your own life as you pursue peace and reconciliation with others. You will find a deeper passion for peace when you have "tasted and seen that the Lord is good" (Psalm 34:8), because you will want the same for others.

Invite God to search your heart, seeking out any areas of sin that need to be addressed. Be very honest with Him, and allow Him to be honest with you. You may even find a trusted friend to confess to, as part of the biblical process of reconciliation. Read the Scriptures below, and make room for the peace of Jesus that will fill your heart as He cleanses your sin and heals your brokenness.

O taste and see that the Lord is good;
How blessed is the man who
takes refuge in Him!

PSALM 34:8

Search me, O God, and know my heart;
Try me and know my anxious thoughts;
And see if there be any hurtful way in me,
And lead me in the everlasting way.

PSALM 139:23-24

I, the Lord, search the heart,
I test the mind,
Even to give to each man
according to his ways,
According to the results of his deeds.

JEREMIAH 17:10

Therefore, confess your sins to one another, and pray for one another so that you may be healed. The effective prayer of a righteous man can accomplish much.

JAMES 5:16

And the peace of God, which surpasses all comprehension, will guard your hearts and your minds in Christ Jesus.

PHILIPPIANS 4:7

DAY 13

The Blood of Jesus

"I will ask the Father, and He will give you another Helper, that He may be with you forever; that is the Spirit of truth, whom the world cannot receive, because it does not see Him or know Him, but you know Him because He abides with you and will be in you."

"I will not leave you as orphans; I will come to you. After a little while the world will no longer see Me, but you will see Me; because I live, you will live also. In that day you will know that I am in My Father, and you in Me, and I in you. He who has My commandments and keeps them is the one who loves Me; and he who loves Me will be loved by My Father, and I will love him and will disclose Myself to him." Judas (not Iscariot) said to Him, "Lord, what then has happened that You are going to disclose Yourself to us and not to the world?" Jesus answered and said to him, "If anyone loves Me, he will keep My word; and My Father will love him, and We will come to him and make Our abode with him. He who does not love Me does not keep My words; and the word which you hear is not Mine, but the Father's who sent Me.

"These things I have spoken to you while abiding with you. But the Helper, the Holy Spirit, whom the Father will send in My name, He will teach you all things, and bring to your remembrance all that I said to you. Peace I leave with you; My peace I give to you; not as the world gives do I give to you. Do not let your heart be troubled, nor let it be fearful."
JOHN 14:16-27

LIVE IT OUT

If you've ever put oil and water into a bowl to mix them, you'll see that they simply will not mix. No matter how much you stir oil and water together, they're going to retract and go back to their old world because oil and water do not like each other. They cannot function in the same space. And then here comes mayonnaise: made up almost entirely of oil and water and, some would say, an absolute necessity for the perfect sandwich. Mayonnaise requires an emulsifier, which is something that takes two opposing objects and pulls them together so they can relate in a way that they could not on their own. In mayonnaise, that emulsifier is eggs. Eggs grab oil and water, pull them together and thicken them into mayonnaise.

When it comes to conflict, our emulsifier is the blood of Jesus. It reaches into each side and pulls us together where we normally would not get along. If you're willing to deal with the sin that causes separation, the blood of Jesus works.

Alford Nobel created dynamite. His intentions were awesome when he created it: He wanted an explosive that could move rock to build roads and get things out of the way to build buildings. He wanted a force that would make life better. Unfortunately, people started using his invention for destructive purposes. Dr. Nobel was distraught. So he took nine million dollars and put it into an account, awarding people who were promoting peace. We call it the Nobel Peace Prize today, of course. Dr. Nobel was motivated by the fact that what he had intended for good was being used for evil. He wanted to award those whose intentions were toward peace, as his were.

God looks for people who instead of making war are making peace using His method of the blood of Christ. And those He calls His own sons and daughters.

REFLECTIONS

1 How does a peacemaker view a conflict, and what do they do about it?

2 How does the blood of Christ affect a conflict, if we let it?

When Dr. Nobel's invention was used for war, did he focus on eradicating war or on promoting peace?

How might your thoughts, perspectives, actions, and words change if you were to focus entirely on promoting peace and inviting the blood of Jesus into your own and others' conflicts?

"

GOD LOOKS FOR PEOPLE WHO INSTEAD OF MAKING WAR **ARE MAKING PEACE** USING HIS METHOD OF THE BLOOD OF CHRIST. AND THOSE HE CALLS HIS OWN SONS AND DAUGHTERS.

CHALLENGE

There are so many ways to promote peace in areas of conflict. Every Christ-centered, covenant marriage made and fought for is promoting unity instead of divorce, without badmouthing or fighting against divorce. Every child birthed, adopted, fostered, mentored, fed, clothed, and cared about is promoting life. Every critical conversation is promoting peace in the workplace, church, or home.

God has given us the Holy Spirit, the carrier of peace, to guide us. Consider the issues or conflicts that stir your heart. Pray, and write down several ways you could speak out *for* peace instead of speaking out *against* conflict. You can even start in your own home, with conflict around chores not being done or two personalities that regularly clash. Ask the Holy Spirit for creative strategies to promote peace.

These things I have spoken to you, so that in Me you may have peace. In the world you have tribulation, but take courage; I have overcome the world.
JOHN 16:33

But now in Christ Jesus you who formerly were far off have been brought near by the blood of Christ.
EPHESIANS 2:13

Now the God of peace, who brought up from the dead the great Shepherd of the sheep through the blood of the eternal covenant, even Jesus our Lord, equip you in every good thing to do His will, working in us that which is pleasing in His sight, through Jesus Christ, to whom be the glory forever and ever. Amen.
HEBREWS 13:20-21

If we walk in the Light as He Himself is in the Light, we have fellowship with one another, and the blood of Jesus His Son cleanses us from all sin.
I JOHN 1:7

Words Matter

Let no unwholesome word proceed from your mouth, but only such a word as is good for edification according to the need of the moment, so that it will give grace to those who hear. Do not grieve the Holy Spirit of God, by whom you were sealed for the day of redemption. Let all bitterness and wrath and anger and clamor and slander be put away from you, along with all malice. Be kind to one another, tender-hearted, forgiving each other, just as God in Christ also has forgiven you.
EPHESIANS 4:29-32

So then we pursue the things which make for peace and the building up of one another.
ROMANS 14:19

Therefore encourage one another and build up one another, just as you also are doing.
I THESSALONIANS 5:11

But speaking the truth in love, we are to grow up in all aspects into Him who is the head, even Christ, from whom the whole body, being fitted and held together by what every joint supplies, according to the proper working of each individual part, causes the growth of the body for the building up of itself in love.
EPHESIANS 4:15-16

LIVE IT OUT

Every school playground reverberates with the old adage, "Sticks and stones may break my bones, but words will never hurt me." Well, that is just a lie. Most people you know, and probably you yourself, have been destroyed by something said to you at a certain time in life. Maybe it was a parent who said, "You're not going to amount to anything." Maybe it was an employer who told you you're no good at your job. Maybe it was a racial or identity slur that made you self-conscious about who you are. The reality is, words do matter because words affect how you think, feel, and ultimately act. If a judge comes in and says, "Guilty" or "Not Guilty," those words matter because they affect your destiny. If a doctor comes in and says, "Benign" or "Malignant," those words do matter. They affect your well-being.

What you say and how you say it—even *when* you say it—affects whether you are building someone up or tearing them down. It is a lifelong process to learn. One day, a lady came to her pastor and said, "Pastor, I want to lay my tongue on the altar." The pastor said, "I'm sorry, but our altar is not that big." It's a joke, but in truth, when it comes to giving our communication to God, that's not often something we're willing to do.

Scripture says that our speech reveals our character. If you are a destructive speaker, constantly tearing down, constantly using profanity, constantly gossiping or slandering, the Bible says that's because there is something wrong with you on the inside.

Your mouth reveals your heart.

A husband and wife were driving down the road one day and passed a paddock of mules. The husband said, "Look, it's a bunch of your relatives." The wife replied, "I know, by marriage." When you look at some of the ways that words are used to unravel people's lives, in the biggest and smallest ways, you come to realize that we all have dynamite in our dentures. We speak with explosive power for good—or for bad. We can construct with dynamite and we can destroy with dynamite. God wants us to understand that the job of the mouth is to build and not destroy.

REFLECTIONS

1 Think of a time when words were used to tear you down. How did they affect you?

2 Think of a time when words were used to build you up. How did they affect you?

How might gossip, profanity, or slander hurt another person who hears?

How might building words help a person who hears, even if those words aren't about them?

“

YOUR MOUTH REVEALS YOUR HEART.

CHALLENGE

Become someone who talks about people behind their backs—but in a good way. Instead of looking for sympathy by telling about all of the wrongs your spouse, children, friends, or coworkers have done to you, talk about the good you see in them. That doesn't mean you can't process or tell about your experiences. But do so with the goal of growth in mind. When you talk with the intention of healing, and listen with the intention of understanding, then a whole lot of relationship and personal growth can happen.

Intentionally "tell on" three people in your life today. But only tell the good. Does your spouse regularly act courageously for the sake of your family? Is your child working hard in a subject that challenges them? Did that store associate offer thoughtful customer service? Make a point of using your words to build something lasting and kingdom-minded.

Therefore, laying aside falsehood, speak truth each one of you with his neighbor, for we are members of one another.
EPHESIANS 4:25

It is foolish to belittle one's neighbor; a sensible person keeps quiet.
PROVERBS 11:12 NLT

Let love be without hypocrisy. Abhor what is evil; cling to what is good.
ROMANS 12:9

A soothing tongue is a tree of life,
But perversion in it crushes the spirit.
PROVERBS 15:4

DAY 15

Between the Posts

Let not many of you become teachers, my brethren, knowing that as such we will incur a stricter judgment. For we all stumble in many ways. If anyone does not stumble in what he says, he is a perfect man, able to bridle the whole body as well. Now if we put the bits into the horses' mouths so that they will obey us, we direct their entire body as well. Look at the ships also, though they are so great and are driven by strong winds, are still directed by a very small rudder wherever the inclination of the pilot desires. So also the tongue is a small part of the body, and yet it boasts of great things.

See how great a forest is set aflame by such a small fire! And the tongue is a fire, the very world of iniquity; the tongue is set among our members as that which defiles the entire body, and sets on fire the course of our life, and is set on fire by hell. For every species of beasts and birds, of reptiles and creatures of the sea, is tamed and has been tamed by the human race. But no one can tame the tongue; it is a restless evil and full of deadly poison. With it we bless our Lord and Father, and with it we curse men, who have been made in the likeness of God; from the same mouth come both blessing and cursing. My brethren, these things ought not to be this way. Does a fountain send out from the same opening both fresh and bitter water? Can a fig tree, my brethren, produce olives, or a vine produce figs? Nor can salt water produce fresh.

JAMES 3:1-12

LIVE IT OUT

The Bible says that when we communicate with each other as Christians, we are to speak the truth in love. Like footballs, our words when we kick them should go through the two goalposts of truth and love. We are to speak the truth to the other person, knowing that we are looking out for their well-being.

Some people major on the truth. They say, "I'm going to tell them what the truth is because even if they can't handle it, they need to hear it." But truth without love becomes dead orthodoxy: it may be true, but there's no life in it. Without love, you are speaking dead words, even if they are true! Conversely, love without truth is empty sentimentalism. It's making a person feel good, but they're not better off for it because it's not the truth.

If you don't tell a person the truth, you don't help. But if you tell the truth without caring about the person, they may be worse off because they're reacting more to you than to the information you gave.

Connect the truth with love, and a person gets the right information with the right heart.

Speaking the truth in love builds a person up and does not tear down, even if the information they're receiving is negative, because truth, with love, is designed to correct and not condemn. It makes a person recognize your desire to help them. And when they know you're aiming to correct AND to help, then the information can reach the heart.

Speaking the truth is one goalpost. Speaking in love is the other. Aim those words right in the middle, and they will build up and not tear down.

REFLECTIONS

1. Think of a time when someone tried to tell you something important but their delivery lacked compassion. How did that conversation go?

2. Think of a time when you shared a tough truth with another person and they received it well. What elements of that conversation made it go well?

Do you believe there is ever a time to tell a hard truth with vehemence and without love? Why or why not?

Describe a situation in today's world that you believe people treat with compassion but not truth.

"

CONNECT THE TRUTH WITH LOVE, AND A PERSON GETS THE RIGHT INFORMATION WITH THE RIGHT HEART.

CHALLENGE

The next time you experience a situation where you'd like to tell the truth to someone about their behavior, ask God first to see that person with His eyes. Try to put yourself in the other person's shoes, to see and feel what they are seeing and feeling. Remember, people are rarely trying to act vindictively or hurtfully. Most likely, they are experiencing things very differently than you and trying to act according to what they understand. Treat their hearts and their well-being like the valuable treasures that they are—as though you were the ring-bearer at a very expensive wedding.

Approach the person with an open heart, allowing the Holy Spirit to adjust your perspective. Then speak in a way that communicates your love and concern for the other. Make sure they know you find value in them, telling them the good you see in them before you tell the truth in love. Aim those words right between the goalposts, and then trust God to carry them through.

Little children, let us not love with word or with tongue, but in deed and truth.

I JOHN 3:18

Sanctify them in the truth;
Your word is truth.

JOHN 17:17

These are the things which you should do: speak the truth to one another; judge with truth and judgment for peace in your gates.

ZECHARIAH 8:16

Lead me in Your truth and teach me,
For You are the God of my salvation;
For You I wait all the day.

PSALM 25:5

DAY 16

Seasoned Speech

Devote yourselves to prayer, keeping alert in it with an attitude of thanksgiving; praying at the same time for us as well, that God will open up to us a door for the word, so that we may speak forth the mystery of Christ, for which I have also been imprisoned; that I may make it clear in the way I ought to speak. Conduct yourselves with wisdom toward outsiders, making the most of the opportunity. Let your speech always be with grace, as though seasoned with salt, so that you will know how you should respond to each person.
COLOSSIANS 4:2-6

You are the salt of the earth; but if the salt has become tasteless, how can it be made salty again? It is no longer good for anything, except to be thrown out and trampled under foot by men.
MATTHEW 5:13

Salt is good; but if the salt becomes unsalty, with what will you make it salty again? Have salt in yourselves, and be at peace with one another.
MARK 9:50

The words of a man's mouth
are deep waters;
The fountain of wisdom is
a bubbling brook.
PROVERBS 18:4

LIVE IT OUT

The tongue is like a wrecking ball with an uncanny ability to destroy. The difference is, it can either destroy someone's spirit or destroy the lies of the enemy that are hurting that person's spirit. Words can work both ways. Do you use your tongue to build up or to tear down?

Speech is a ministry because grace is to be administered! Grace is divine, unmerited favor. Unmerited because the person receiving grace may not deserve it. But you and I are to use our tongues and our communication to administer grace.

As a ministry of grace, God will give you the wisdom to know what to say at the right moment, to the right person, about the right situation.

We don't just say empty words to encourage others or use throw-away phrases to put wrongdoers in their places. Colossians 4:6 (NIV) says to "let your conversation be always full of grace, seasoned with salt, so that you may know how to answer everyone." Put some flavor on it. In other words, make yours as tasty as possible and keep the decay away, because that's what salt does—it retards decay. Flavor your communication. Put some seasoning on it. Make it edible and digestible. Don't just say words because you feel them; say words because they are a ministry.

If we start ministering to each other with the goal of building each other up, we'll get less reaction from one another. We'll get less conflict, less competition, and less anger. The ministry of words unites us.

REFLECTIONS

1 Has someone ministered to you through words recently? Describe the situation.

2 In what situations do you find yourself quick to speak? In what situations do you find yourself more apt to listen?

3 Respond to the idea that our words should be seasoned for taste and freshness (no decay).

4 Have you seen the effects of poor words in church? What about seasoned words?

"AS A MINISTRY OF GRACE, GOD WILL GIVE YOU THE WISDOM FOR WHAT TO SAY AT THE RIGHT MOMENT, TO THE RIGHT PERSON, ABOUT THE RIGHT SITUATION.

CHALLENGE

How intentional are you about the words you speak? For some who would be called "external processors," this may be an extra challenge. For others, the "internal processors," they may do a lot of the work on the inside, but what comes out in the end is just as essential.

For one day, pay extra close attention to two things when you speak: the *intentions* of your heart and the *flavor* of your words. Are you speaking with the desire to be heard and found right, or to bless and minister to the person you're talking to? Is your word choice designed to go down easy or to sting a bit? Journal your discoveries: celebrate the times you said edifying things to others, and ask God to refine the areas you need help in. For an extra step, go back and apologize for your words to anyone who received a sharp or selfish tone from you.

Every grain offering of yours, moreover,
you shall season with salt, so that the salt
of the covenant of your God shall not be
lacking from your grain offering; with
all your offerings you shall offer salt.
LEVITICUS 2:13

All the offerings of the holy gifts, which
the sons of Israel offer to the Lord,
I have given to you and your sons
and your daughters with you, as a
perpetual allotment. It is an everlasting
covenant of salt before the Lord to
you and your descendants with you.
NUMBERS 18:19

He went out to the spring of water
and threw salt in it and said, "Thus
says the Lord, 'I have purified these
waters; there shall not be from there
death or unfruitfulness any longer.'"
II KINGS 2:21

There is one who speaks rashly
like the thrusts of a sword,
But the tongue of the wise brings healing.
PROVERBS 12:18

Watch Your Mouth

Therefore be patient, brethren, until the coming of the Lord. The farmer waits for the precious produce of the soil, being patient about it, until it gets the early and late rains. You too be patient; strengthen your hearts, for the coming of the Lord is near. Do not complain, brethren, against one another, so that you yourselves may not be judged; behold, the Judge is standing right at the door. As an example, brethren, of suffering and patience, take the prophets who spoke in the name of the Lord. We count those blessed who endured. You have heard of the endurance of Job and have seen the outcome of the Lord's dealings, that the Lord is full of compassion and is merciful.

But above all, my brethren, do not swear, either by heaven or by earth or with any other oath; but your yes is to be yes, and your no, no, so that you may not fall under judgment.

Is anyone among you suffering? Then he must pray. Is anyone cheerful? He is to sing praises. Is anyone among you sick? Then he must call for the elders of the church and they are to pray over him, anointing him with oil in the name of the Lord; and the prayer offered in faith will restore the one who is sick, and the Lord will raise him up, and if he has committed sins, they will be forgiven him. Therefore, confess your sins to one another, and pray for one another so that you may be healed. The effective prayer of a righteous man can accomplish much.

JAMES 5:7-16

Therefore be imitators of God, as beloved children; and walk in love, just as Christ also loved you and gave Himself up for us, an offering and a sacrifice to God as a fragrant aroma.

But immorality or any impurity or greed must not even be named among you, as is proper among saints; and there must be no filthiness and silly talk, or coarse jesting, which are not fitting, but rather giving of thanks.

EPHESIANS 5:1-4

LIVE IT OUT

God's relationship to you vertically is tethered to how you relate to others horizontally. For example, I Peter 3:7 says that if a husband isn't treating his wife right (horizontally), he shouldn't even bother to get on his knees (vertically), because God is not listening. That is a strong connection! So many times we wonder why it seems that God is not answering our prayers. He says to us that it's because He sees how we're treating our brothers and sisters—and it's a family affair. What we say to one another, and how we say it, is a spiritual issue.

So often the destructive words we use are due to the condition of our hearts. We are struggling or hurting, so our words struggle and hurt too. There is good news in James 5:8. When you are patient instead of piercing, when you remain strong instead of slanderous, you can rest in the knowledge that the coming of the Lord is near. You're going through a rough time, you need God to help. He is closer than you think. Verse 9 says don't complain against one another so that you will avoid judgment, because the Judge is standing right at the door.

In other words, in your patience the Lord is near. But if you complain, He will come through that door and judge you for it. And the big difference is your mouth!

Watch your mouth, because your mouth may be blocking your blessing.

Instead, pray. Sing. Encourage. Call on others. Confess. Forgive. Heal. Use your mouth for the benefit of others, for the furthering of God's kingdom, and for your own benefit.

REFLECTIONS

How does what you think affect what you say?

How do we speak to or about others? How does God speak to us? How do the two compare?

What adjustments might you want to make to your attitude toward others and what comes out of your mouth?

What answers are you currently seeking from God? Does your prayer feel "blocked" or just "in the waiting room" with Him?

“

WATCH YOUR MOUTH, BECAUSE YOUR MOUTH MAY BE BLOCKING YOUR BLESSING.

CHALLENGE

Only God can reveal any areas in our hearts and thoughts that need His attention. And the good thing is, He really does care about our hurts and disappointments, our brokenness, and the things we don't understand. There are so many root reasons that our methods of communication might need refinement, and if we are serious about a lifestyle of seeking God, it's rarely because we are deliberately trying to be mean.

Read the last paragraph of today's devotional thought again, and then read James 5:13-16 again. Find something to sing about, something to pray about, something to thank God for, something to confess, and something to forgive. Fill today with life-giving speech, to the best of your ability. Every time you choose God's way with words, the world (and your own heart) grows exponentially brighter.

Let the peace of Christ rule in your hearts, to which indeed you were called in one body; and be thankful.
COLOSSIANS 3:15

Rejoice always; pray without ceasing; in everything give thanks; for this is God's will for you in Christ Jesus. Do not quench the Spirit.
I THESSALONIANS 5:16-19

If I speak with the tongues of men and of angels, but do not have love, I have become a noisy gong or a clanging cymbal.
I CORINTHIANS 13:1

Let the words of my mouth and
the meditation of my heart
Be acceptable in Your sight,
O Lord, my rock and my Redeemer.
PSALM 19:14

Be Encouraged

"This is the covenant that I
will make with them
After those days," says the Lord:
"I will put My laws upon their heart."
HEBREWS 10:16

Since we have confidence to enter the holy place by the blood of Jesus, by a new and living way which He inaugurated for us through the veil, that is, His flesh, and since we have a great priest over the house of God, let us draw near with a sincere heart in full assurance of faith, having our hearts sprinkled clean from an evil conscience and our bodies washed with pure water. Let us hold fast the confession of our hope without wavering, for He who promised is faithful.
HEBREWS 10:19-23

Be patient, brethren, until the coming of the Lord. The farmer waits for the precious produce of the soil, being patient about it, until it gets the early and late rains.
JAMES 5:7

Therefore let us draw near with confidence to the throne of grace, so that we may receive mercy and find grace to help in time of need.
HEBREWS 4:16

Draw near to God and He will draw near to you.
JAMES 4:8

LIVE IT OUT

On October 24, 1929, the stock market crashed, leading to the Great Depression. Lives were turned upside down. Thirty-seven thousand businesses went belly up. The unemployment rate zoomed to 24 percent nationwide. Suicide and divorce skyrocketed because people were desperate.

Today, many are living in their own great depression. Life has been unfair. Because of a difficult relationship, or a vice that has seemingly conquered them, or overwhelm, or a career breakdown, they have lost sight of hope. Men and women of the Bible were depressed and discouraged too. From Job to Jonah to John, men and women fought to believe God's promises.

The book of Hebrews addresses Jewish Christians who wanted to give up. The author says to them, *Don't go back. I know you want to, I know you feel like it, I know you think it's not worth it to keep going. Seems like this Christianity thing isn't working. But don't stop! Don't turn around! Don't quit.* We can relate, can't we? If we're telling the whole truth, sometimes we feel, *This Jesus thing is not working. The Bible doesn't seem real and church is not making a difference. I'm not seeing a payoff for my faith*

Hebrews tells us of the new covenant—an agreement God made with us, a covering—that allows us to draw near to Him, not to go back but to go forward! The author of Hebrews says to boldly enter into the presence of the living God, not casually but with some oomph to it!

Today people are looking for connection through Twitter, Facebook, and all kinds of chat rooms so that they can relate to somebody. People are desperate for somebody to listen to them. And Jesus is saying, "You're dealing with all these somebodies, but I'm right here in charge of the throne room. You want to connect? I've opened up a way where every man and woman who has come to faith alone in the finished work of Jesus Christ has a basis for connection."

You have an access code for connection.

You are invited to draw near. If you are discouraged, the temptation is to shrink away and get out. But Jesus says to come close and come in. The time you don't feel like making contact with heaven is exactly when you should.

REFLECTIONS

Why is it important for you to be encouraged by truth before encouraging others?

What do you do when you are discouraged? Is your first instinct to run toward Jesus or away from Him? Why?

When you are lonely, do you turn first to social media, to friends or family, or to God?

In your own words, how does the New Covenant affect your access to God?

"

YOU HAVE AN ACCESS CODE FOR CONNECTION.

CHALLENGE

If you've ever been on an airplane, you know that the attendant makes an announcement at the beginning of a flight. Part of the instructions includes what to do in case of a drop in cabin pressure. Oxygen masks will drop from the ceiling, the attendant says. Make sure to place your own mask over your nose and mouth before you assist your child or anyone around you who needs help. Why? Because if you were to lose consciousness while trying to help, you would be good to no one. Likewise, it's important to understand where our hope comes from before you assist others in understanding hope.

Your challenge today is to read Hebrews chapter 10. Ask God all the questions you need to. Find a concordance app and look up the Greek or Hebrew origins of key words in the passage. Then in your own words, write out what access to the throne means. Think of times you've leaned on God in discouragement. Think of times you've seen His promises fulfilled in your own life. Dwell on His goodness and the beauty of the blood of Jesus. Then when it comes time to encourage someone else, you will have your own experiences and wisdom to draw from.

Why are you in despair, O my soul?
And why have you become
disturbed within me?
Hope in God, for I shall again praise Him
For the help of His presence.
O my God, my soul is in despair within me;
Therefore I remember You from
the land of the Jordan
And the peaks of Hermon,
from Mount Mizar.
Deep calls to deep at the
sound of Your waterfalls;
All Your breakers and Your
waves have rolled over me.
The Lord will command His
lovingkindness in the daytime;
And His song will be with me in the night,
A prayer to the God of my life.

I will say to God my rock, "Why
have You forgotten me?
Why do I go mourning because of
the oppression of the enemy?"
As a shattering of my bones,
my adversaries revile me,
While they say to me all day
long, "Where is your God?"
Why are you in despair, O my soul?
And why have you become
disturbed within me?
Hope in God, for I shall yet praise Him,
The help of my countenance and my God.

PSALM 42:5-11

Cheerleaders

Let us consider how to stimulate one another to love and good deeds, not forsaking our own assembling together, as is the habit of some, but encouraging one another; and all the more as you see the day drawing near.
HEBREWS 10:24-25

And we know that God causes all things to work together for good to those who love God, to those who are called according to His purpose. For those whom He foreknew, He also predestined to become conformed to the image of His Son, so that He would be the firstborn among many brethren; and these whom He predestined, He also called; and these whom He called, He also justified; and these whom He justified, He also glorified.

What then shall we say to these things? If God is for us, who is against us?
ROMANS 8:28-31

We urge you, brethren, admonish the unruly, encourage the fainthearted, help the weak, be patient with everyone.
I THESSALONIANS 5:14

"For I know the plans that I have for you," declares the Lord, "plans for welfare and not for calamity to give you a future and a hope. Then you will call upon Me and come and pray to Me, and I will listen to you. You will seek Me and find Me when you search for Me with all your heart."
JEREMIAH 29:11-13

LIVE IT OUT

God knows that we are subject to discouragement in life. It happens to everyone. So He tells us to encourage one another. In Hebrews 10:24, we are prompted to reflect on or devise ways to invigorate or spur others onward. One of the main reasons you join a church body is not just for the singing or the preaching, but for the stimulation you get from other believers. The verse says to stimulate *one another*. That's not pulpit to pew, but pew to pew. Everyone in the church, on every given day, should serve as either a source of encouragement or a recipient of encouragement, motivating one another to keep going in the faith.

In sports, the job of the cheerleaders is to support the team. Whether things are going bad or great on the field, cheerleaders cheer toward victory. They don't grumble and gossip when the team is struggling. No, whether there is a bad call, a bad play, a fumble, or an interception, cheerleaders are for the team, not the performance.

The greatest cheerleaders should be found in the house of God. Not because they necessarily agree with the performance of a person, but because they are supporting the person. They want to see you reverse the score and move the momentum. Nobody needs people on the side telling them they're failing, or that there are better people out there for the job. You need somebody who, on your worst day, is still on your side. That's what encouragement does!

In the Greek, the word for encouragement means to come alongside to help, strengthen, or support.

When left alone, discouraged people go back. They remove themselves further from the promises of God. To keep them from going back, you need to consider how to motivate them forward. Only by drawing near to the Lord do you draw near to His promise of the fulfillment of His purpose in your life.

REFLECTIONS

What types of behaviors, attitudes, or words motivate you the most?

Have you ever been encouraged by someone else to "keep the faith"? In what way?

What are some of the barriers to motivating others?

Do you agree that it is part of the job of the people in church to stimulate one another toward good works? Why or why not?

“

IN THE GREEK, THE WORD FOR ENCOURAGEMENT MEANS TO COME ALONGSIDE TO HELP, STRENGTHEN, OR SUPPORT.

CHALLENGE

There is no shortage of discouragement these days. In your church, your news feed, your work, or your family, people are struggling. But if you knew you had tools to help encourage them to keep going, would you use them?

Find three ways to motivate others toward love and good deeds this week. It might be as simple as a social media post. It might be more personal, like inviting a friend over for coffee and listening to her heart, then encouraging her to use her gifts. Plan out the ways you will be a cheerleader to other believers, just as cheerleaders practice their cheers. As a bonus move, if you yourself are feeling discouraged, tell someone who you know loves God and will help you find ways to keep going.

Bright eyes gladden the heart;
Good news puts fat on the bones.
PROVERBS 15:30

And we know that God causes all things to work together for good to those who love God, to those who are called according to His purpose.
ROMANS 8:28

Now may the God who gives perseverance and encouragement grant you to be of the same mind with one another according to Christ Jesus, so that with one accord you may with one voice glorify the God and Father of our Lord Jesus Christ.
ROMANS 15:5-6

For just as the sufferings of Christ are ours in abundance, so also our comfort is abundant through Christ.
II CORINTHIANS 1:5

Lifting Up with Love

For whatever was written in earlier times was written for our instruction, so that through perseverance and the encouragement of the Scriptures we might have hope. Now may the God who gives perseverance and encouragement grant you to be of the same mind with one another according to Christ Jesus, so that with one accord you may with one voice glorify the God and Father of our Lord Jesus Christ. Therefore, accept one another, just as Christ also accepted us to the glory of God.

ROMANS 15:4-7

Above all, love each other deeply, because love covers over a multitude of sins.

I PETER 4:8 NIV

By this all people will know that you are My disciples: if you have love for one another.

JOHN 13:35 NASB

Two are better than one because they have a good return for their labor. For if either of them falls, the one will lift up his companion. But woe to the one who falls when there is not another to lift him up. Furthermore, if two lie down together they keep warm, but how can one be warm alone? And if one can overpower him who is alone, two can resist him. A cord of three strands is not quickly torn apart.

ECCLESIASTES 4:9-12

Follow God's example, therefore, as dearly loved children and walk in the way of love.

EPHESIANS 5:1-2 NIV

LIVE IT OUT

When it comes to encouraging one another, God asks you to find others to lift up. When you do, you are not only connecting with others, but you are connecting with Him as well. But if you are going to be a cheerleader for God, you can't just be doing your own thing on the field while all the others are moving together. Strengthening others in the Lord involves truth and love. True encouragement fits between those two goalposts. You never negate God's standard of truth, but you do it in a way that says, "I see you, I care about you, and I'm here to come alongside you and help."

You could use a hammer and call it the truth. But if somebody is in a hole, they don't need another person to come with a shovel and start digging dirt to bury them. They need a rope.

Encouragement involves using the appropriate tools of truth, based on the situation and the person, to lift them up.

If you're listening to people who won't give you God's point of view, then they will keep you in regression. If a man is walking away from his family because he can't handle the pressure, he doesn't need guy friends telling him it's the right thing to do for whatever reason. He needs a bunch of brothers to surround him and say, "Hang in there, kingdom man. Rise to the occasion. Get back in there, and we're going to hang with you. Your kids need you, and your wife needs you too, even if you don't feel her support."

Ladies don't need girlfriends who will say, "You don't need him, you have a career, no need to submit to a man." Unbiblical advice is a straight-up lie, and that is regression. Your girlfriends are taking you away from the promise.

People who encourage are going to tell you God's standard, but through loving you and seeking your well-being. And when you become that kind of encourager yourself, you are drawing people toward hope.

REFLECTIONS

1 Do you tend to lean more toward telling the truth without love or showing compassion without truth? What do you think causes you to lean that direction?

2 Have you experienced a friendship or relationship where they led you away from the truth? How did that relationship end—or is it continuing?

3 How do you feel about gossip and slander (putting someone else down)? Pretty harmless, or pretty destructive?

4 Do you have friends who tell you the truth in love and receive truth in love from you? How have those relationships benefited you?

"

ENCOURAGEMENT INVOLVES USING THE APPROPRIATE TOOLS OF TRUTH, BASED ON THE SITUATION AND THE PERSON, TO LIFT THEM UP.

CHALLENGE

We can't control how others are going to behave, but we can evaluate our own behavior and make beneficial changes. We can also decide who is a part of our closer circles of friends and loved ones. If we want to grow in the Lord, we need healthy, devoted, God-seeking relationships in our lives. We need to hear the truth and be able to speak it, with both love and compassion.

Evaluate the quality of the relationships in your life. If there are any relationships that repeatedly bring you down, decide whether you should have a conversation with the person or take a few steps back from the relationship. Make a special point of thanking those people in your life who have modeled biblical encouragement. And be open to any person this week who comes to you needing encouragement. Ask God to help you with just the right words and wisdom.

But one who looks intently at the perfect law, the law of liberty, and abides by it, not having become a forgetful hearer but an effectual doer, this man will be blessed in what he does.
JAMES 1:25

Let no unwholesome word proceed from your mouth, but only such a word as is good for edification according to the need of the moment, so that it will give grace to those who hear.
EPHESIANS 4:29

Bear one another's burdens, and thereby fulfill the law of Christ.
GALATIANS 6:2

We urge you, brethren, admonish the unruly, encourage the fainthearted, help the weak, be patient with everyone.
I THESSALONIANS 5:14

DAY 21

Love Is Kind

Therefore if there is any encouragement in Christ, if there is any consolation of love, if there is any fellowship of the Spirit, if any affection and compassion, make my joy complete by being of the same mind, maintaining the same love, united in spirit, intent on one purpose. Do nothing from selfishness or empty conceit, but with humility of mind regard one another as more important than yourselves; do not merely look out for your own personal interests, but also for the interests of others. Have this attitude in yourselves which was also in Christ Jesus, who, although He existed in the form of God, did not regard equality with God a thing to be grasped, but emptied Himself, taking the form of a bond-servant, and being made in the likeness of men. Being found in appearance as a man, He humbled Himself by becoming obedient to the point of death, even death on a cross. For this reason also, God highly exalted Him, and bestowed on Him the name which is above every name, so that at the name of Jesus every knee will bow, of those who are in heaven and on earth and under the earth, and that every tongue will confess that Jesus Christ is Lord, to the glory of God the Father.

So then, my beloved, just as you have always obeyed, not as in my presence only, but now much more in my absence, work out your salvation with fear and trembling; for it is God who is at work in you, both to will and to work for His good pleasure.

Do all things without grumbling or disputing; so that you will prove yourselves to be blameless and innocent, children of God above reproach in the midst of a crooked and perverse generation, among whom you appear as lights in the world, holding fast the word of life, so that in the day of Christ I will have reason to glory because I did not run in vain nor toil in vain.

PHILIPPIANS 2:1-16

LIVE IT OUT

God expects His people to be ambassadors of kindness. He doesn't just want you to be nice, He wants you to be kind. Nice can be your persona. Nice can be your personality. Kindness is your action. You can be nice just because you're nice, but that doesn't mean you exercise kindness. Kindness is what you do with your niceness because if you're just nice to yourself, you may not be kind to others.

Kindness is niceness on public display.

People ought to know how nice you are by how kindly you talk, walk, and act. So this should be our mindset. We are to be penetrating the culture with a different atmosphere. Some years ago in our Education Center, one of the restrooms had a continuous putrid smell. Great time and effort and money were spent trying to find out why this smell was lasting so long. Finally we brought in a professional team to figure it out. We paid them to discover and solve the problem of why this stench was leaving the restroom and creating a funk in the building. One of our custodial staff who happened to go into the restroom one day noticed something very simple: The fan in the ceiling was turning the wrong way. So instead of pushing stuff out, it was driving stuff in. All he did was turn the fan the right way and the expensive, stinky problem was solved.

The culture is filled with people turned the wrong way, creating chaos and vitriol, and all the money and programs will not change things unless we turn.

If Jesus were selfish, no one would be saved. But He left His rightful place in heaven, and His love reached out through the sacrifice of Christ and the gift of the cross. God isn't against self-interest. But if you are only concerned about how you are doing, you are a cul-de-sac Christian instead of a conduit saint.

Love is kind. If you're unkind, you do not love. If you're mean to your children, you aren't loving them. You don't love your mate if you're cursing them. Love doesn't put down or reduce dignity. Love is kind, and kindness is niceness in action, not in words only.

REFLECTIONS

1 In your own words, describe the difference between being nice and being kind.

2 Describe how you talk, walk, and act. Describe how you think others see you. Do you think your kindness is penetrating the culture?

3 Name some ways you can help people turn the right way.

4 Do you agree that you cannot be unkind and love someone at the same time?
Why or why not?

5 What is the most recent kindness you can think of, by either you or by someone else?

"KINDNESS IS NICENESS ON PUBLIC DISPLAY.

CHALLENGE

When Jesus said He is, and then we are, the light of the world, He made a powerful illustration about the effect we can have on the world around us. In a dark room, any light—even the tiniest match flame—takes darkness away. It's impossible for darkness to eliminate light. Light always wins. Similarly, a kind act will always cancel evil. Even when there is no obvious meanness, kindness advances the kingdom of heaven.

Step out today with a heart toward adding kindness. If you see meanness, ambivalence, pain, or sadness, simply show love. It could be a smile or a word that you offer, or something more elaborate. Make it a goal to surprise three people with kindness today. Journal about your experience.

Love is patient, love is kind and
is not jealous; love does not
brag and is not arrogant.

I CORINTHIANS 13:4

But love your enemies, and do good, and lend, expecting nothing in return; and your reward will be great, and you will be sons of the Most High; for He Himself is kind to ungrateful and evil men.

LUKE 6:35

If anyone wants to sue you and take your shirt, let him have your coat also. Whoever forces you to go one mile, go with him two. Give to him who asks of you, and do not turn away from him who wants to borrow from you.

You have heard that it was said, "You shall love your neighbor and hate your enemy." But I say to you, love your enemies and pray for those who persecute you, so that you may be sons of your Father who is in heaven.

MATTHEW 5:40-45

In everything, therefore, treat people the same way you want them to treat you.

MATTHEW 7:12

DAY 22

Most Effective

But to each one is given the manifestation of the Spirit for the common good.
I CORINTHIANS 12:7

For even as the body is one and yet has many members, and all the members of the body, though they are many, are one body, so also is Christ. For by one Spirit we were all baptized into one body, whether Jews or Greeks, whether slaves or free, and we were all made to drink of one Spirit.

For the body is not one member, but many. If the foot says, "Because I am not a hand, I am not a part of the body," it is not for this reason any the less a part of the body. And if the ear says, "Because I am not an eye, I am not a part of the body," it is not for this reason any the less a part of the body. If the whole body were an eye, where would the hearing be? If the whole were hearing, where would the sense of smell be? But now God has placed the members, each one of them, in the body, just as He desired. If they were all one member, where would the body be? But now there are many members, but one body. And the eye cannot say to the hand, "I have no need of you"; or again the head to the feet, "I have no need of you." On the contrary, it is much truer that the members of the body which seem to be weaker are necessary; and those members of the body which we deem less honorable, on these we bestow more abundant honor, and our less presentable members become much more presentable, whereas our more presentable members have no need of it. But God has so composed the body, giving more abundant honor to that member which lacked, so that there may be no division in the body, but that the members may have the same care for one another. And if one member suffers, all the members suffer with it; if one member is honored, all the members rejoice with it.

Now you are Christ's body, and individually members of it.
I CORINTHIANS 12:12-27

LIVE IT OUT

What does it mean to be a member of a church? It is the decision to be identified and functionally involved with a body of Christians who are learning together to live under the lordship of Jesus Christ. It doesn't mean simply showing up and occupying space. It means to show up and grow up in a group together. You can only maximize your relationship to God by attachment to others.

Your vertical relationship, or that with God, is directly correlated to your horizontal relationship with others.

If you are detached from the body, there will be a breakdown in the flow of God's life in your own. If I chop off my hand and put it over there, the fact that my hand is located in the same building with my body will be meaningless both for my hand and for my body. Both of us lose. My hand loses because it doesn't get the benefit of the rest of me. But the rest of me loses because I don't get the benefit of my hand. I am going to be limited in my body if my hand is disconnected, even if it is in the vicinity. So, just doing things that make you appear to be a Christian doesn't mean you are benefiting from Jesus. You must be connected to the life around you.

In First Corinthians 12:7 we are told that each of us is given "the manifestation of the Spirit for the common good." The Spirit is like the blood flowing through the body or like the nerves of the body. He transfers God's life to the various parts of the body. But guess what? If my hand is cut off from my arm, it doesn't get the transfer of life. So God moves through connection.

God wants every Christian to be a functionally identified part of a local body of Christians, so that they can get the benefit of the vertical along with the horizontal. Then the full expression of God can be experienced throughout the body. In other words, the church needs you as much as you need the church.

REFLECTIONS

1 What are your views on church membership?

2 Do you see yourself and your gifts as a necessary part of the body of Christ? Why or why not?

3 Name Christians in your life on whom you can depend. What gifts do they each possess?

Describe a time when you felt deeply connected to a group of other believers.

List some of your gifts as a way you can serve the body of Christ.

“YOUR VERTICAL RELATIONSHIP, OR THAT WITH GOD, IS DIRECTLY CORRELATED TO YOUR HORIZONTAL RELATIONSHIP WITH OTHERS.

CHALLENGE

The idea of becoming a member of a local church has become a little old-fashioned to some. In other areas of the church, membership has taken a turn away from biblical reasons and toward more self-serving ones. But the heart behind membership is a commitment to a certain group with a common goal: seeking, serving, and growing in Christ together. When you commit to a certain portion of the body of Christ, and they commit to you, then you gain accountability, assistance, partnership, friendship, and probably most importantly, a stronger ministry unto Him.

If you are not committed to a local church, commit to yourself to find one. It will not be a perfect place. Just ask God where He wants you. If you are a part of a local group of believers, then commit to be more involved. Check your heart to see if you have treated the church as a consumer treats a store, where you come and get something for your money. Then look for ways to use your gifts for the good of the kingdom inside the church.

For through the grace given to me I say to everyone among you not to think more highly of himself than he ought to think; but to think so as to have sound judgment, as God has allotted to each a measure of faith. For just as we have many members in one body and all the members do not have the same function, so we, who are many, are one body in Christ, and individually members one of another.

ROMANS 12:3-5

Bear one another's burdens, and thereby fulfill the law of Christ. For if anyone thinks he is something when he is nothing, he deceives himself.

GALATIANS 6:2-3

Now I urge you, brethren, keep your eye on those who cause dissensions and hindrances contrary to the teaching which you learned, and turn away from them.

ROMANS 16:17

DAY 23

Preferences

Now accept the one who is weak in faith, but not for the purpose of passing judgment on his opinions. One person has faith that he may eat all things, but he who is weak eats vegetables only. The one who eats is not to regard with contempt the one who does not eat, and the one who does not eat is not to judge the one who eats, for God has accepted him. Who are you to judge the servant of another? To his own master he stands or falls; and he will stand, for the Lord is able to make him stand.

One person regards one day above another, another regards every day alike. Each person must be fully convinced in his own mind. He who observes the day, observes it for the Lord, and he who eats, does so for the Lord, for he gives thanks to God; and he who eats not, for the Lord he does not eat, and gives thanks to God. For not one of us lives for himself, and not one dies for himself; for if we live, we live for the Lord, or if we die, we die for the Lord; therefore whether we live or die, we are the Lord's. For to this end Christ died and lived again, that He might be Lord both of the dead and of the living.

But you, why do you judge your brother? Or you again, why do you regard your brother with contempt? For we will all stand before the judgment seat of God. For it is written, "As I live, says the Lord, every knee shall bow to Me, and every tongue shall give praise to God." So then each one of us will give an account of himself to God.

Therefore let us not judge one another anymore, but rather determine this—not to put an obstacle or a stumbling block in a brother's way. I know and am convinced in the Lord Jesus that nothing is unclean in itself; but to him who thinks anything to be unclean, to him it is unclean. For if because of food your brother is hurt, you are no longer walking according to love. Do not destroy with your food him for whom Christ died. Therefore do not let what is for you a good thing be spoken of as evil; for the kingdom of God is not eating and drinking, but righteousness and peace and joy in the Holy Spirit.

ROMANS 14:1-17

LIVE IT OUT

My late father-in-law did not celebrate Christmas. He believed that (1) we didn't know for sure it was Christ's birthday; and (2) it had become so secular a holiday that it didn't carry the meaning the day should have. He didn't see Christmas as a time to worship Christ anymore but a time to exchange presents, so he wouldn't celebrate Christmas. So my wife didn't grow up celebrating Christmas; they celebrated New Year's Day instead. Now, I don't have a problem with Christmas. I grew up with it, our kids grew up with it, but we did not try to force my father-in-law to celebrate it with us because it was against his conscience. So we celebrated New Year's with him every year. We listened to his desires and honored him.

There is no Bible verse that says, "Worship Me on My birthday." The Bible says you're free to have and act on your own preferences! So many of the things we fuss and fight about within the church today have to do with preferential confusion. Some Christians don't dance, for example. The problem is, you can't go to Scripture to argue that point, because worshipful dancing is in the Bible. But the Bible does say, if you are free to do something, you should not judge somebody who's not free to do it, and you shouldn't try to force them.

Legalism is where you either take God's law and expect it to do what it was never designed to do, or create human laws and make them sound like God. In fact, the nature of a cult is to come up with rules and laws that do not come from the Word of God but hold you hostage to obey them.

What we get to do, as Christians, is listen to one another and honor one another's consciences and preferences.

That doesn't mean we should ever compromise our own conscience before God. But we should accept one another's preferences within the design of God's kingdom because each one of us is on our own journey of learning to be free.

REFLECTIONS

What are some things you have learned are "wrong" or "frowned upon" in the church?

Write down the biblical basis for each of the above.

3 How does one's conscience play into the way that he or she lives for Jesus?

4 Are there any disagreements within your own family or friend groups regarding preferences? How have they been handled?

“

WHAT WE GET TO DO, AS CHRISTIANS, IS LISTEN TO ONE ANOTHER AND HONOR ONE ANOTHER’S CONSCIENCES AND PREFERENCES.

CHALLENGE

Sometimes it's hard to distinguish between what God wants for us and what our own preferences are. Our consciences can be tricky like that. If someone chooses not to watch certain movies, but others watch them without issue, you might be left wondering, *What's right? What should I do? How does God feel about it?* Or if you feel strongly about drinking, tattoos, or piercings, and someone you know strongly disagrees with you—can you still be friends? The answer is yes, but how that plays out will take effort, deference, and respect.

Seek out one person this week to talk about an issue or area you two disagree on. Search the Bible first for God's heart on the matter. Then ask questions with the intention of understanding. Don't approach the conversation with any plans to change minds. Just listen. Share your point of view if asked. But decide to accept the other person's desire to honor God the way they've chosen to.

Do not judge, and you will not be judged; and do not condemn, and you will not be condemned; pardon, and you will be pardoned.

LUKE 6:37

For there is no partiality with God.

ROMANS 2:11

Now may the God who gives perseverance and encouragement grant you to be of the same mind with one another according to Christ Jesus, so that with one accord you may with one voice glorify the God and Father of our Lord Jesus Christ.

Therefore, accept one another, just as Christ also accepted us to the glory of God.

ROMANS 15:5-7

Let Freedom Ring

Do not judge so that you will not be judged. For in the way you judge, you will be judged; and by your standard of measure, it will be measured to you. Why do you look at the speck that is in your brother's eye, but do not notice the log that is in your own eye? Or how can you say to your brother, "Let me take the speck out of your eye," and behold, the log is in your own eye? You hypocrite, first take the log out of your own eye, and then you will see clearly to take the speck out of your brother's eye.

MATTHEW 7:1-5

Do not judge according to appearance, but judge with righteous judgment.

JOHN 7:24

What then shall we say to these things? If God is for us, who is against us? He who did not spare His own Son, but delivered Him over for us all, how will He not also with Him freely give us all things?

ROMANS 8:31-32

LIVE IT OUT

The church is made up of different people with different histories, backgrounds, and desires. If we're going to live truly free, then we're going to have to learn to accept one another.

Accepting one another can transform families and churches. Moreover, many families and churches don't make it because they never get around to accepting one another. In fact, there are many Christians whose fulltime job is to critique and change one another! If we spent less time trying to change our mates and more time accepting them, there would be much less conflict. We need to embrace the fact that every Christian is on his or her own journey toward freedom.

A man came from a foreign country. He was very nervous because it was ten minutes to six, and as he hailed a taxi, he said, "Please get me to my hotel by six! Hurry!" He was operating according to his old country, where a military regime demanded a six o'clock curfew or people would be arrested. The man had not learned to operate in freedom yet, even though he was in a free country.

Many people who accept Christ bring old unregenerate thinking into their new country, and they haven't learned what it means to be free yet. So what do you do? You take them to the hotel. You don't fight them, because they've got to learn what freedom is for themselves.

Some people were saved out of situations. They don't dance anymore, because dancing for them meant the club, and the club meant drinking and being picked up. So dancing is more than dancing, it's a whole lifestyle that they are avoiding for now. If you force them to dance, you force them to sin—not because dancing is wrong, but because their association of it is wrong.

The Bible says one thing about dress: "Be modest"—don't overdress or underdress. Don't call inappropriate attention to yourself. Now, once you're modest, you can pick the colors and styles you like. And if you don't like it, don't wear it! People are free to like their style, within the context of the biblical guideline.

Accepting others means letting freedom ring within the walls of biblical context.

We love people by allowing them to walk their own road as they seek Jesus. Kindness sometimes means putting our own preferences on the back burner, even when we are right.

REFLECTIONS

1 Do you have a hard time letting others be themselves? If so, why do you think that is? If not, why do you think it's easy for you?

2 When you have a strong conviction about something and someone else disagrees, how do you treat them?

3 Is judging others ever okay? Why or why not?

4 How does accepting others benefit the church in general?

5 How do others' preferences affect your own freedom?

"

ACCEPTING OTHERS MEANS LETTING FREEDOM RING WITHIN THE WALLS OF BIBLICAL CONTEXT.

CHALLENGE

It can be harder than you think to operate on your convictions when others disagree. You may have experienced this yourself, if you feel convicted about something that most Christians—or even most of the rest of the world—don't understand. To that end, it can mean the world to someone when another person supports them in their beliefs.

Go to bat for someone who needs it. At an event with someone who does not drink? Make them a special fruity nonalcoholic beverage. Have a friend who doesn't watch R-rated movies? Stand with her when the rest of the group wants to see something she can't. Know someone who feels convicted about gossip? Steer the conversation toward something different if your friends or family start talking about someone else. Even if you don't have similar convictions, your kindness will not go unnoticed.

He has told you, O man, what is good;
And what does the Lord require of you
But to do justice, to love kindness,
And to walk humbly with your God?
MICAH 6:8

Bear one another's burdens, and
thereby fulfill the law of Christ.
GALATIANS 6:2

Therefore, accept one another,
just as Christ also accepted
us to the glory of God.
ROMANS 15:7

Learn to do good;
Seek justice,
Reprove the ruthless,
Defend the orphan,
Plead for the widow.
ISAIAH 1:17

DAY 25

Comfort Has a Purpose

Blessed be the God and Father of our Lord Jesus Christ, the Father of mercies and God of all comfort, who comforts us in all our affliction so that we will be able to comfort those who are in any affliction with the comfort with which we ourselves are comforted by God. For just as the sufferings of Christ are ours in abundance, so also our comfort is abundant through Christ. But if we are afflicted, it is for your comfort and salvation; or if we are comforted, it is for your comfort, which is effective in the patient enduring of the same sufferings which we also suffer; and our hope for you is firmly grounded, knowing that as you are sharers of our sufferings, so also you are sharers of our comfort.

II CORINTHIANS 1:3-7

When you pass through the
waters, I will be with you;
And through the rivers, they
will not overflow you.
When you walk through the fire,
you will not be scorched,
Nor will the flame burn you.
For I am the Lord your God.

ISAIAH 43:2-3

Therefore we do not lose heart, but though our outer man is decaying, yet our inner man is being renewed day by day. For momentary, light affliction is producing for us an eternal weight of glory far beyond all comparison, while we look not at the things which are seen, but at the things which are not seen; for the things which are seen are temporal, but the things which are not seen are eternal.

II CORINTHIANS 4:16-18

LIVE IT OUT

On January 10, 2003, a young Burmudian man named Robert Lambe floated in the ocean for twenty hours without his boat after it capsized. For twenty hours he treaded water, staring a death sentence in the face. All of a sudden, a helicopter was overhead. It radioed the USNS *Comfort* on its way to the Persian Gulf. The ship veered out of its way to deliver one man, and the doctor on board nursed Robert back to health.

Sometimes we find ourselves treading water, and we don't know how much longer we can hang in there. Our legs and arms get tired, but if we look up, hovering over us is the Deliverer. At just the right time, the God of all comfort will make sure that the comfort we need comes our way.

When you look like you're facing certain defeat, the Father is monitoring the earth, looking for others of His children to take you on board. And there is a Physician to bring you around; He is the God of all comfort. Your greatest growth won't come merely from your deliverance but from God joining you in your pain. He didn't deliver the three Hebrew boys out of the fire; He joined them in the fire. Because that's when you know He is real.

God allows your affliction, and comforts you there, so that He can use you as an agent of comforting somebody else in their affliction. It's one thing to stand up, even with a Bible in your hand, and tell people what God can do. But it's a whole different ball game when you've been there and you're talking not simply out of your biblical knowledge but out of your life experience.

It's one thing to be able to quote a Scripture. It's another thing to have lived the Scripture you're quoting.

God allows you to go through afflictions, and allows you to be comforted, because He knows there is an opportunity coming your way. And who can listen with understanding, encourage, and support a person more than somebody else who's been where they have been and seen God do what He can do?

REFLECTIONS

How has God delivered and comforted you in the past?

Name a person, time, or situation in which you were comforted by someone who had been through the same circumstances as you.

Name a person, time, or situation in which you were able to comfort someone because you had been through a similar situation in the past.

4 What is a Scripture that you can quote with experience and certainty behind it?

5 Are you waiting for comfort now? In what ways?

"

IT'S ONE THING TO BE ABLE TO QUOTE A SCRIPTURE. IT'S ANOTHER THING TO HAVE LIVED THE SCRIPTURE YOU'RE QUOTING.

CHALLENGE

Going through hard things is no fun. But knowing that God can use every bit of pain and trouble that He allows, in order to benefit both you and the people around you, can ease the suffering to a degree.

Spend some time journaling about people in your life who are experiencing challenges. It may be one of your kids going through something at school, or a friend facing trouble. As you pray for them, pay close attention to the situations that you yourself have experienced. Put yourself in their shoes, using your own experiences to guide you. You may be in the perfect position to reach out to them and offer comfort. Comfort doesn't require answers; it simply offers hope. Whose shoulders need your arm wrapped around them today, and how has God primed you for this moment?

Indeed, we had the sentence of death within ourselves so that we would not trust in ourselves, but in God who raises the dead.
II CORINTHIANS 1:9

He will wipe away every tear from their eyes; and there will no longer be any death; there will no longer be any mourning, or crying, or pain; the first things have passed away.
REVELATION 21:4

I would have despaired unless
I had believed that I would see
the goodness of the Lord
In the land of the living.
PSALM 27:13

These things I have spoken to you, so that in Me you may have peace. In the world you have tribulation, but take courage; I have overcome the world.
JOHN 16:33

DAY 26

Designed to Comfort

In You, O Lord, I have taken refuge;
Let me never be ashamed;
In Your righteousness deliver me.
Incline Your ear to me, rescue me quickly;
Be to me a rock of strength,
A stronghold to save me.
For You are my rock and my fortress;
For Your name's sake You will
lead me and guide me.
You will pull me out of the net which
they have secretly laid for me,
For You are my strength.
Into Your hand I commit my spirit;
You have ransomed me, O Lord,
God of truth.
PSALM 31:1-5

The eyes of the Lord are
toward the righteous
And His ears are open to their cry.
PSALM 34:15

The things you have learned and received and heard and seen in me, practice these things, and the God of peace will be with you.
PHILIPPIANS 4:9

For you were called to freedom, brethren; only do not turn your freedom into an opportunity for the flesh, but through love serve one another. For the whole Law is fulfilled in one word, in the statement, "You shall love your neighbor as yourself."
GALATIANS 5:13-14

Bear one another's burdens, and thereby fulfill the law of Christ.
GALATIANS 6:2

LIVE IT OUT

Go to the country or to your grandma, and they'll tell you that you don't really ever need to go to the doctor because they have natural, time-tested, and approved remedies. They'll say, "Save your money, child, we can take care of this here and now." And the reason they go to their own cabinets first is because they've been there before. They've had the pain, seen the pain, and worked with the pain. The doctor is only called in when what has worked before is not working this time.

In this era of self-help and proficiency, everyone thinks they can solve it all on their own. But head knowledge is different from heart knowledge, and love requires heart. Right here among the body of Christ, there are home remedies for stuff you've seen before because you've been there. You've felt that. Who can minister better to a woman who has lost her baby than another mother who has grieved? Who can minister to somebody struggling with cancer better than somebody else who has been there and seen God comfort them as they wrestled with the disease? Who better to minister to help somebody who has lost a parent than a child who has lost their parent and experienced God's comfort? In other words, God has allowed you to go through afflictions and comforted you in yours. Don't limit that to yourself because it wasn't just for you.

He comforts you so you can comfort others.

I got a box with something shipped to us, and it had all this packing material in it to cushion what was inside so it wouldn't roll around. Our stuff was protected and kept from damage because the box was well-insulated. When I had to mail something to someone else, I didn't get a new box—I used the one that had been sent to me. I let the cushioning I received be the cushioning I shared.

God wants you to not only receive His comfort but to share His comfort. He wants people to come into the family of God who are running on empty, and find fuel from other believers. Grace enough to share.

REFLECTIONS

1 What are some home remedies or life hacks you utilize in your family?

2 What is a home remedy or life hack that someone has shared with you? How did it change your level of happiness or relief?

3 When was the last time you sat with someone in their pain, not offering advice but just offering the ministry of your presence?

4 Do you have a lot to offer the hurting? Why or why not?

“
HE COMFORTS
YOU SO YOU
CAN COMFORT
OTHERS.

CHALLENGE

Sometimes it's hard to see opportunities to bless others because we don't see ourselves as a blessing. Or we see someone facing challenging circumstances, but our own wounds keep us from offering comfort because we feel that we still need to be comforted for what we went through.

Are you holding onto pain that the Lord is asking you to let go of? Are you dealing with unforgiveness or a situation you haven't reconciled between yourself and God? It's so important, for your own relationship with Him and then for your relationships with others, to allow Him to address and dress your wounds. Be as real with yourself and with Him as you can, and trust Him to heal you. When you truly find freedom and hope in your own situation, you will be able to confidently and joyfully share that comfort with others in their need.

But in all these things we overwhelmingly conquer through Him who loved us. For I am convinced that neither death, nor life, nor angels, nor principalities, nor things present, nor things to come, nor powers, nor height, nor depth, nor any other created thing, will be able to separate us from the love of God, which is in Christ Jesus our Lord.

ROMANS 8:37-39

Be anxious for nothing, but in everything by prayer and supplication with thanksgiving let your requests be made known to God. And the peace of God, which surpasses all comprehension, will guard your hearts and your minds in Christ Jesus.

PHILIPPIANS 4:6-7

But I rejoiced in the Lord greatly, that now at last you have revived your concern for me; indeed, you were concerned before, but you lacked opportunity.

PHILIPPIANS 4:10

DAY 27

Authorized to Hear

And Jesus returned to Galilee in the power of the Spirit, and news about Him spread through all the surrounding district. And He began teaching in their synagogues and was praised by all. And He came to Nazareth, where He had been brought up; and as was His custom, He entered the synagogue on the Sabbath, and stood up to read. And the book of the prophet Isaiah was handed to Him. And He opened the book and found the place where it was written,

"The Spirit of the Lord is upon Me,
Because He anointed Me to
preach the gospel to the poor.
He has sent Me to proclaim
release to the captives,
And recovery of sight to the blind,
To set free those who are oppressed,
To proclaim the favorable
year of the Lord."

And He closed the book, gave it back to the attendant and sat down; and the eyes of all in the synagogue were fixed on Him. And He began to say to them, "Today this Scripture has been fulfilled in your hearing."

LUKE 4:14-21

For I am not ashamed of the gospel, for it is the power of God for salvation to everyone who believes.

ROMANS 1:16

LIVE IT OUT

Have you ever called a company on the telephone to fix some problem in your home? You call the company, and to the person who answers you spill the beans; you tell them everything that's wrong and that needs to be taken care of. And after you've poured your heart out, they pass you on to somebody else because they're not the one to handle it. That's a frustrating thing, to pour your heart out and then to hear, "You need to talk to somebody else." They switch you to another person, who listens to your whole story again and tells you they're not the right department either. After a while, you're going to say to them, "Now look. I need you to pass me on to somebody authorized to address this, because the rest of you folk are wasting my time."

A lot of people are wasting their time because they're going to unauthorized personnel for deliverance in life. They're going to people just because they pick up the phone—they think they are the ones to solve their problem. But Jesus says, *I have come with good news because I have been duly authorized to be the reversal of your circumstances.*

In Luke 4, Jesus went to the synagogue on the day of worship. It was the habit those days when you had a visiting teacher or rabbi to allow them to do the homily that day. So they invited Him to speak, and it says He opened the scroll and "found the place"—which means, what He was going to read was on purpose.

Jesus offers good news to poor, captive, blind, and oppressed people. He brings the year of the Lord's favor on people. He is the fulfillment of every promise of God.

As a Christian, you are authorized to hear the broken stories of the hurting and oppressed. You have the right answer, because you have Jesus. You never need to turn someone away or pass the buck. That doesn't mean there won't be times you can help somebody find further assistance, as needed. But the good news starts with you.

REFLECTIONS

1 How comfortable are you with sharing the gospel?

2 How do you feel when someone starts talking about their problems with you?

Do you feel "authorized" to listen to others in their pain? Why or why not?

Who first told you about Jesus?

"

JESUS OFFERS GOOD NEWS TO POOR, CAPTIVE, BLIND, AND OPPRESSED PEOPLE. HE BRINGS THE YEAR OF THE LORD'S FAVOR ON PEOPLE. HE IS THE FULFILLMENT OF EVERY PROMISE OF GOD.

CHALLENGE

First Peter 3:15 says that we should always be "ready to make a defense to everyone who asks you to give an account for the hope that is in you." It doesn't mean you need to have a debate-ready argument or to take an apologetics class (although there would be nothing wrong with that). But it does mean that as believers, we are responsible to understand what we believe and why we believe it, to the point that we can share with others in their need.

Challenge yourself to write out your reason for Jesus. Make it personal and simple: Think of the man in John 9:25 who said, "I do not know; one thing I do know, that though I was blind, now I see." Your story is your testimony that led you to Him and can benefit others in doing the same.

How lovely on the mountains
Are the feet of him who brings good news,
Who announces peace
And brings good news of happiness,
Who announces salvation,
And says to Zion, "Your God reigns!"
ISAIAH 52:7

And we preach to you the good news of the promise made to the fathers, that God has fulfilled this promise to our children in that He raised up Jesus, as it is also written in the second Psalm, "You are My Son; today I have begotten You."
ACTS 13:32-33

While he was still speaking, a bright cloud overshadowed them, and behold, a voice out of the cloud said, "This is My beloved Son, with whom I am well-pleased; listen to Him!"
MATTHEW 17:5

DAY 28

Works and the Word

And He called the twelve together, and gave them power and authority over all the demons and to heal diseases. And He sent them out to proclaim the kingdom of God and to perform healing.
LUKE 9:1-2

Whatever city you enter and they receive you, eat what is set before you; and heal those in it who are sick, and say to them, "The kingdom of God has come near to you."
LUKE 10:8-9

These twelve Jesus sent out after instructing them: "Do not go in the way of the Gentiles, and do not enter any city of the Samaritans; but rather go to the lost sheep of the house of Israel. And as you go, preach, saying, 'The kingdom of heaven is at hand.' Heal the sick, raise the dead, cleanse the lepers, cast out demons. Freely you received, freely give."
MATTHEW 10:5-8

But you will receive power when the Holy Spirit has come upon you; and you shall be My witnesses both in Jerusalem, and in all Judea and Samaria, and even to the remotest part of the earth.
ACTS 1:8

LIVE IT OUT

There is a relationship between doing good work that helps the lives of people and giving the good Word that changes the destiny of people. The good work gives validity to the good Word. The good work is helpful, but it's not just so that you make people have a better life; it's so that you help them to have a better life toward an eternal home. Good things are good, but we have a bigger agenda.

Jesus said to His disciples in Luke 9:2 and 10:9 that they should go out and heal the sick while preaching the kingdom. Our job is to do both.

Our good works open hearts to receive the good Word.

When a hungry man receives a sandwich from you, his heart is opened to hear the witness from your mouth. If you tell him you want to win him for heaven but that you don't care about his history, then you've convoluted the message because the testimony of the action must fit the invitation of the message. If you've been born again, then God is expecting you to touch the lives of others.

When I was a young boy and had not yet learned to swim, I somehow drifted to the deep end of a pool. I began struggling, gurgling water, trying to push myself up to send a message for help. My friend Donald was sitting on the edge of the pool, and finally, he saw me going under. He was older and could swim. Donald jumped into the water and delivered me. I was jumping as hard as I could, but I could not deliver myself because the circumstances were just too deep. But there was somebody in my vicinity who had an ability I did not possess, who reached in and delivered me. Donald was good news in a bad situation!

From that point, I decided to learn how to swim. I never wanted to be in that situation again. After I learned to swim, I became a lifeguard, and finally a water safety instructor. So having been delivered from certain death, I got to the point where I could save others and train others to save others.

God has reached down and saved you, and He doesn't want you to go back to where He has delivered you from. He wants you to become a spiritual lifeguard, finding others who need to be delivered and discipling others to do the same.

REFLECTIONS

1 Can you pinpoint a moment when you were born again? Write about it.

2 Is it easy for you to show kindness to others in Jesus' name? Or easier to be kind without bringing Jesus into it? Why do you think one is easier than the other?

Where are you on the spectrum from newly saved, to saving others, to discipling others to save others?

How has sharing Jesus gone for you in the past? Have you been encouraged or discouraged by it?

“ OUR GOOD WORKS OPEN HEARTS TO RECEIVE THE GOOD WORD.

CHALLENGE

Is it time to up your game? If you have been a believer for any length of time, you are in a position to show others Christ. You have something they don't—something they need. And you have the most fantastic tool for opening the door to that conversation: kindness.

If you have never shared Jesus with someone, there's no shame in it. Look for an opportunity to share your kindness with a stranger or loved one, and be prepared to attribute the good work to a good God. If you are nervous about having the right words, look up some Scriptures (there are tons of resources online) and know your own testimony since no one can dispute that! Your courage to share Jesus may just be enough to save someone's life.

What use is it, my brethren, if someone says he has faith but he has no works? Can that faith save him? If a brother or sister is without clothing and in need of daily food, and one of you says to them, "Go in peace, be warmed and be filled," and yet you do not give them what is necessary for their body, what use is that? Even so faith, if it has no works, is dead, being by itself.

But someone may well say, "You have faith and I have works; show me your faith without the works, and I will show you my faith by my works."

JAMES 2:14-18

DAY 29

Relationship

He is before all things, and in Him all things hold together. He is also head of the body, the church; and He is the beginning, the firstborn from the dead, so that He Himself will come to have first place in everything. For it was the Father's good pleasure for all the fullness to dwell in Him, and through Him to reconcile all things to Himself, having made peace through the blood of His cross; through Him, I say, whether things on earth or things in heaven.

And although you were formerly alienated and hostile in mind, engaged in evil deeds, yet He has now reconciled you in His fleshly body through death, in order to present you before Him holy and blameless and beyond reproach—if indeed you continue in the faith firmly established and steadfast, and not moved away from the hope of the gospel that you have heard.

COLOSSIANS 1:17-23

We are no longer to be children, tossed here and there by waves and carried about by every wind of doctrine, by the trickery of men, by craftiness in deceitful scheming; but speaking the truth in love, we are to grow up in all aspects into Him who is the head, even Christ, from whom the whole body, being fitted and held together by what every joint supplies, according to the proper working of each individual part, causes the growth of the body for the building up of itself in love.

EPHESIANS 4:14-16

LIVE IT OUT

Have you ever been hammering something and missed? That's not a pleasant feeling. I did that once, and all heaven broke loose. Lord have mercy! The hammer missed and hit my finger, which sent a message to my brain, "We're hurting down here!" My brain sent a message to my mouth, "Tell everybody else we're hurting!" My brain told my other hand, "Drop the hammer, and grab the finger to bring comfort! Help it, help it!"

My hand didn't need a program or instruction book. It didn't even need a Bible. Out of relationship, my hand immediately went into action, showing concern for another member of my body. But it only did that because there was connection. My feet didn't go visit a book on *What Do Feet Do when a Finger Is in Pain*? They walked to the ice chest for a cold pack, all by themselves, because of connection.

A lot of times, we use the Bible as an excuse not to be connected. We say we need to understand the Bible better first. But when there is connection, Bible is built in. Connection helps us understand the application of the Bible to the body.

The next time you work on a puzzle, pay close attention. A mass of stuff on the surface looks disconnected, but you will notice protrusions and indentations, and when you get the right piece connected with a different piece, where they were made to connect, then you come up with a picture that makes sense.

When you get believers with indentations and protrusions that match up and connect with one another, you have a picture of God Almighty, through His connected body, the church.

Connection among the body leads to a portrayal of Jesus and the Word to the world.

REFLECTIONS

1 Do you agree that as believers, we are directly tied to and dependent on other believers? Why or why not?

2 Do you believe that relationship can demonstrate the Bible, or that understanding the Bible is required before true relationship happens? Why or why not?

3 Describe a time when someone's "protrusion" fit well with your "indentation" and you became connected.

Do you believe that relationship with other believers is required in order to serve others well? Why or why not?

What are the benefits of living in community with other believers?

"

CONNECTION AMONG THE BODY LEADS TO A PORTRAYAL OF JESUS AND THE WORD TO THE WORLD.

CHALLENGE

If you are committed to a particular church, then there is a place for you in it. You may already be serving in fulfilling ways, participating in small groups and events, and showing up every Sunday. Or perhaps you are not. As we have explored today, the most important part of membership to a body is relationship.

Evaluate the relationships you have with others in your church. Do they know you authentically? Do you know others authentically and make room for true connection? Challenge yourself to meet one new person at church this week, and look for common ground. Dig a little deeper with those you're already connected to. Specifically look for ways that your relationships, serving groups, and ministries paint a true picture of Jesus for anyone who sees.

And this is eternal life, that they may
know You, the only true God, and
Jesus Christ whom You have sent.

JOHN 17:3 NASB

And He gave some as apostles, and some
as prophets, and some as evangelists,
and some as pastors and teachers, for
the equipping of the saints for the work
of service, to the building up of the
body of Christ; until we all attain to the
unity of the faith, and of the knowledge
of the Son of God, to a mature man,
to the measure of the stature which
belongs to the fullness of Christ.

EPHESIANS 4:11-13

For even as the body is one and yet has
many members, and all the members
of the body, though they are many,
are one body, so also is Christ.

I CORINTHIANS 12:12

DAY 30

Meek Makes Room

Blessed are the poor in spirit, for
theirs is the kingdom of heaven.

Blessed are those who mourn,
for they shall be comforted.

Blessed are the gentle, for they
shall inherit the earth.

Blessed are those who hunger
and thirst for righteousness,
for they shall be satisfied.

Blessed are the merciful, for
they shall receive mercy.

Blessed are the pure in heart,
for they shall see God.

Blessed are the peacemakers, for
they shall be called sons of God.

Blessed are those who have been
persecuted for the sake of righteousness,
for theirs is the kingdom of heaven.

Blessed are you when people insult
you and persecute you, and falsely
say all kinds of evil against you
because of Me. Rejoice and be glad,
for your reward in heaven is great;
for in the same way they persecuted
the prophets who were before you.

MATTHEW 5:3-12

Have this attitude in yourselves which was also in Christ Jesus, who, although He existed in the form of God, did not regard equality with God a thing to be grasped, but emptied Himself, taking the form of a bond-servant, and being made in the likeness of men. Being found in appearance as a man, He humbled Himself by becoming obedient to the point of death, even death on a cross. For this reason also, God highly exalted Him, and bestowed on Him the name which is above every name, so that at the name of Jesus every knee will bow, of those who are in heaven and on earth and under the earth, and that every tongue will confess that Jesus Christ is Lord, to the glory of God the Father.

PHILIPPIANS 2:5-11

Remind them to be subject to rulers, to authorities, to be obedient, to be ready for every good deed, to malign no one, to be peaceable, gentle, showing every consideration for all men.

TITUS 3:1-2

LIVE IT OUT

When most people hear the words "meek" or "gentle," they don't like it. Meekness sounds a lot like weakness. But really, meekness is a superpower.

Meekness is power under control.

The Greek word for meek is *praos*, and it refers to domesticated animals. A greyhound wearing his little coat and walking calmly on his leash alongside his owner is the same dog that won the race last week and could beat any other dog in a race at that moment. Meekness is not a loss of power or strength but of that power under control. Meekness is submission to the master.

First Peter 3 verse 5 says to a wife that if she is not meek, her husband won't change. If she is trying to change him by being out of control, he won't get better. Meekness is God's way of bringing humility into our lives as we submit to legitimate spiritual authority. A meek person bows low before God so they can stand tall among men. A meek person makes room for others, listens well, keeps their ego in check, and stays connected to God through the Spirit. Meekness is blessed by God because it acknowledges Him as the one in authority, and gives Him room to speak and act through the one who has submitted their power and strength to His leadership.

When you choose meekness, you allow God to move and others to thrive.

REFLECTIONS

1 When you hear the word *meek*, what does it make you think of?

2 If Jesus showed perfect meekness on the night He was arrested and crucified, how does that change your view of meekness?

Do you find it hard or easy to keep your power under control? This could be your tongue, knowledge, or authority. Consider how you wield the things that you alone manage.

Who in your life regularly demonstrates meekness?

"MEEKNESS IS POWER UNDER CONTROL.

CHALLENGE

One of the most difficult aspects of meekness is that we tend to have a very hard time submitting. Allowing someone else to exercise authority over us can feel triggering, threatening, uncomfortable, and scary. But when done within a biblical context, keeping our strength in check is one of the most advanced and powerful things we can do.

Think of the relationships you have and particularly a relationship that has experienced a recent misunderstanding or difference of opinions. Contact that person and determine to have a conversation with them where you simply listen to their side. Determine not to share your views (unless they ask), but to write notes on what they say. This may be especially hard if it's with a child or someone you normally manage. But the more you can demonstrate meekness before them, the more they will see Jesus.

Like a city that is broken
into and without walls
Is a man who has no control over his spirit.
PROVERBS 25:28 NASB

Therefore, putting aside all filthiness
and all that remains of wickedness, in
humility receive the word implanted,
which is able to save your souls.
JAMES 1:21

But let it be the hidden person of the
heart, with the imperishable quality
of a gentle and quiet spirit, which
is precious in the sight of God.
I PETER 3:4

He leads the humble in justice,
And He teaches the humble His way.
PSALM 25:9

Seek the Lord,
All you humble of the earth
Who have carried out His ordinances;
Seek righteousness, seek humility.
ZEPHANIAH 2:3

ABOUT THE AUTHOR

Dr. Tony Evans is the founder and senior pastor of Oak Cliff Bible Fellowship in Dallas, founder and president of The Urban Alternative, and author of over 150 books, booklets, and Bible studies. The first African American to earn a doctorate of theology from Dallas Theological Seminary, he has been named one of the Twelve Most Effective Preachers in the English-Speaking World by Baylor University. Dr. Evans's radio broadcast is heard on over 1,400 radio outlets daily, and his sermons can be heard online anytime at TonyEvans.org or by downloading the Tony Evans Sermons app.

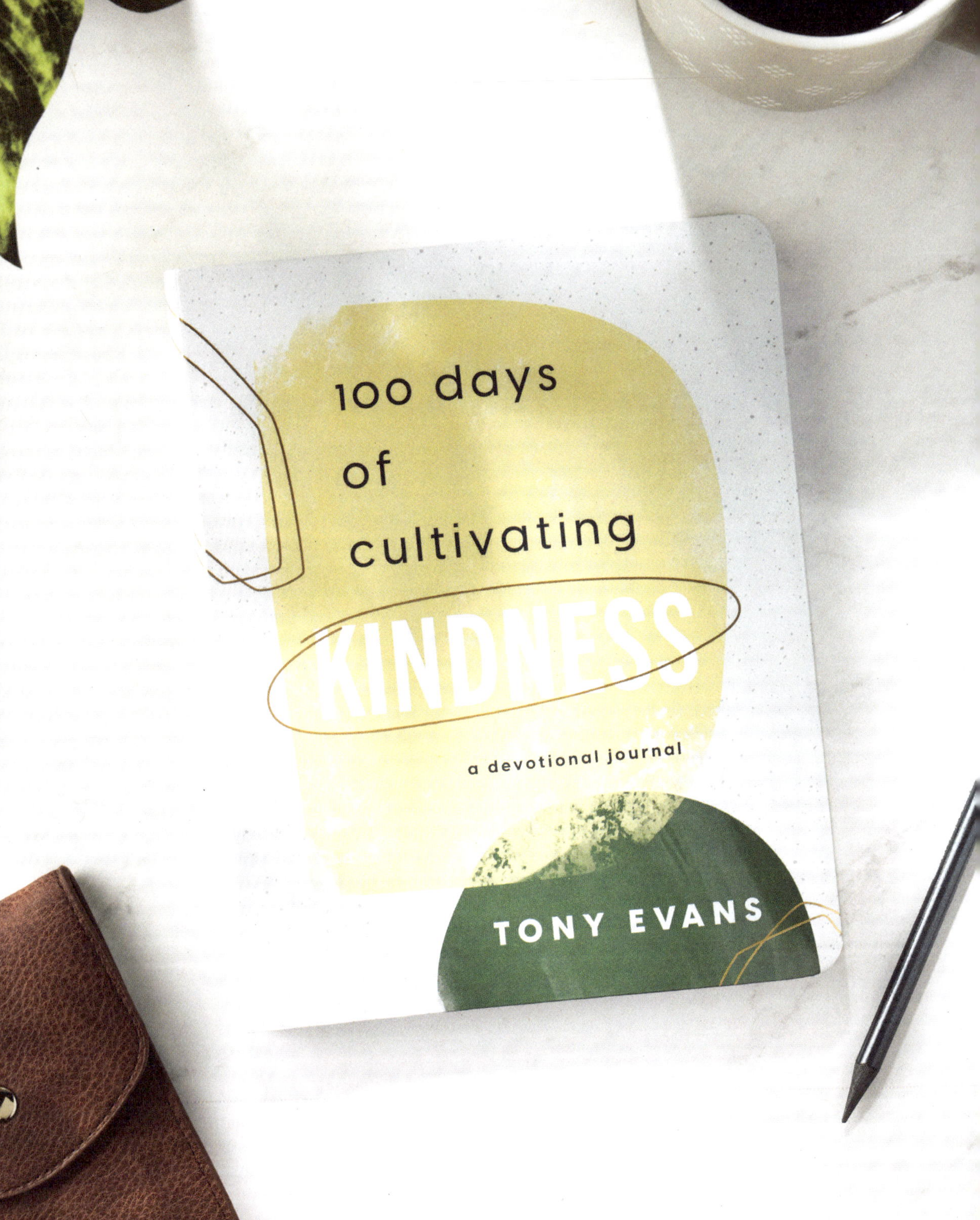

100 days
of
cultivating
KINDNESS
a devotional journal
TONY EVANS

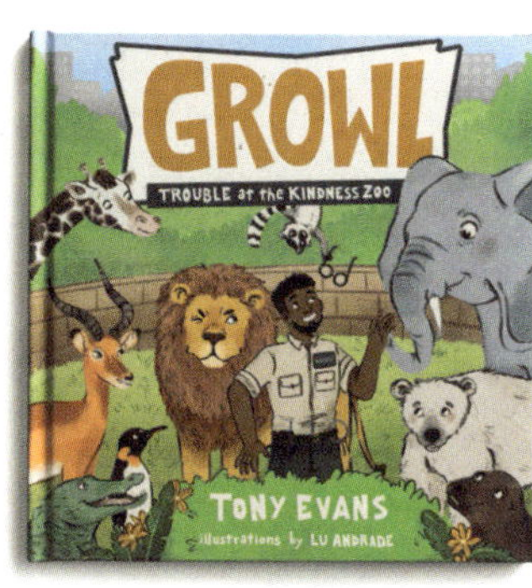

WANT MORE ON HOW TO SPREAD KINDNESS FROM DR. EVANS?

You can find his *Kindness in the Culture* gift collection and more at *dayspring.com* and various retail stores near you.

First Edition, August 2023

Published by:

21154 Highway 16 East
Siloam Springs, AR 72761
dayspring.com

Cover Design by: Brady Voss

Printed in Canada
Prime: U1411
ISBN: 979-8-88602-454-8